CITIZEN *of* HEAVEN

NO WAITING PERIOD REQUIRED

CORNEL RIZEA

Copyright © 2018 by Cornel Rizea
All rights reserved.
ISBN-13: 978-1-7321807-0-3

Unless otherwise indicated, all Scriptures are taken from the New King James Version®. Copyright © 1982 by Thomas Nelson. Used by permission. All rights reserved.

Scripture quotations marked ESV are taken from the ESV® Bible (The Holy Bible, English Standard Version®), copyright © 2001 by Crossway, a publishing ministry of Good News Publishers. Used by permission. All rights reserved.

Scripture quotations marked NIV are taken from the Holy Bible, New International Version®, NIV®. Copyright © 1973, 1978, 1984, 2011 by Biblica, Inc.™ Used by permission of Zondervan. All rights reserved worldwide. www.zondervan.com.

Scripture quotations marked BSB are taken from the Holy Bible, Berean Study Bible, BSB. Copyright ©2016 by Bible Hub. Used by Permission. All Rights Reserved Worldwide.

Scripture quotations marked HCSB are taken from the Holman Christian Standard Bible®, Copyright © 1999, 2000, 2002, 2003, 2009 by Holman Bible Publishers. Used by permission. HCSB® is a federally registered trademark of Holman Bible Publishers.

Scripture quotations marked NASB are taken from the New American Standard Bible® (NASB). Copyright © 1960, 1962, 1963, 1968, 1971, 1972, 1973, 1975, 1977, 1995 by The Lockman Foundation. Used by permission. www.Lockman.org.

Scripture quotations marked NLT are taken from the Holy Bible, New Living Translation, copyright ©1996, 2004, 2015 by Tyndale House Foundation. Used by permission of Tyndale House Publishers, Inc., Carol Stream, Illinois 60188. All rights reserved.

CONTENTS

Foreword by Dr. Donald McKay vii
Preface ix
Introduction xiii

1. Unhidden Agenda 1
2. Rodica 6
3. Backgrounds, Pit Stops, Detours, and Destinations 11
4. Questions 21
5. Creation or Evolution? Only ONE Can Be True 28
6. Sunrise 36
7. Science Fiction or Supernatural Reality 42
8. Seeking Truth—The Origin of Everything 49
9. Value, Purpose, and the Future 56
10. Faith and Foundations 62
11. God's Amazing Love 67
12. Everyday Miracles in Plain Sight 71
13. Profound Courage 75
14. Godlessness 80
15. "Riz" Kids 86
16. Video, Audio, and Thought Recordings 92
17. Forever—It's Critical 97
18. Sarcasm—Offend Someone You Care About 102
19. Application for Citizenship 109

FOREWORD

Cornel Rizea is not a professional writer. By trade he is an engineer. Many non-professionals who venture into writing fail miserably. But this is not the case with Cornel. He has written a *very good* book for a variety of important reasons.

#1 It's a *passionate* book.

Interacting with Cornel, which I have had the privilege of doing for some two decades, is a delight. Yet it can also be deceiving, for underneath that cool reserved demeanor of his beats a passionate heart. This passion comes through as one reads chapter after interesting chapter.

#2 It's a *profound* book.

This is a good read not merely because it reflects the passion of its author but also because of its subject matter. Cornel has written about life's most important questions, namely "Whom am I?"; "Where did I come from?"; and "Where am I going?" As he discusses these issues, he makes a great case for why the Darwinian theory of evolution is simply not credible, thereby becoming a kind of apologist (defender) for special creation. His ultimate purpose in all of this is that individuals might come to know the God of the Bible and might trust exclusively in His Son the Lord Jesus for their salvation.

#3 It's a *personal* book.

Not merely because it recounts a good deal of Cornel's personal history (for example, his birth in Romania, his move to Canada, and the death of his sister), but because of the very personal interest he had in this project, which is his four precious children: Kyle, Kendyl, Kelly, and Katie. In a chapter devoted to them, he writes, "I admit that it was this sense of love and responsibility toward my kids that energized me to keep going during times when I was tempted to simply stop writing. Even though I've wandered away from biblical teaching more times than I care to remember, I want my kids to know that God forgives. I want them to know that no matter what condition they find themselves in, they can never have a more reliable and trustworthy friend than God Himself. My hope is that they all open their hearts to the healing truth of His Word."

Finally, this is a personal book because in it Cornel testifies to his own personal faith in the Lord Jesus and the assurance that he has that he is a citizen of heaven. This citizenship is available to anyone and everyone through faith in the living, loving Christ, the one and only Savior of mankind (Philippians 3:20).

Soli Deo gloria,

Dr. Donald McKay

PREFACE

I want you to benefit from this book, period. I want you to look deep inside yourself and really know for sure that when your life on earth ends, your eternal soul will be in heaven. If, on the other hand, you're simply not sure, then I want you to promise yourself you won't give up searching until you have no more doubt. Your peace of mind gained from knowing this is my #1 motivating reason for writing.

I respect and understand that many things in life are trying to capture your attention. However, when you look in the mirror, honestly ask yourself, "Am I sure of my final destiny?" I encourage you to seek the truth; you will soon discover your next steps.

I have made the following statement many times during the past thirty years or so: "It's okay not to know something, but it's *not* okay to remain in that state of ignorance." Mostly, I have said this during my career as a mechanical engineer when searching for resolutions to problems. However, the significance of these same words increases exponentially when it comes to the topic of heaven and hell. Honestly, how versed are you on this subject?

The Bible tells us there is a Day of Judgment we will all face (see Hebrews 9:27). No one will stand with you, and you will be the only one allowed to speak on your behalf—if you can muster the courage. Your memory will be triggered like never before—your mind is created to record *every* event in your life—and you will know for sure that the Day of Judgment is a very serious matter. You will not have a lawyer by your side, nor the right to make one last phone call for anyone to come to your defense.

The idea of personal accountability seems to be less and less popular in society these days; nobody welcomes the idea of being questioned about anything we think, say, or do. After all, we live in a free country and it's nobody else's business what we do, say, or think, or so we reason. If we sense the slightest difference of opinions coming our way, our built-in defense mechanisms kick into overdrive. If challenged in any way, we try to explain and defend our position or actions, including inappropriate behaviors and choices. We are much closer to going over the proverbial edge than finding a place of calm order and inner peace.

Every day, we're busy juggling life's activities to the best of our abilities, while stressful situations persist all around. But taking a little time to gain understanding by looking at our own situation from a higher perspective can reveal the real problem we all face.

Through this book, I want to help you realize that the eternal Creator of the universe is seeking your heart and He wants you to seek Him out as well. The Creator Himself knows you personally and He wants you to learn about Him as well, for your own good; He wants to give you a better life on earth and ultimately grant you access into heaven.

It's no coincidence that you somehow came across this little book. I daresay that you were meant to find it, just as much as I was meant to share these words with you at this point in our lives. Right about now, you might be tempted to discount the expression *everything happens for a reason*. Admittedly, there was a time when I used to be in that same camp as well; it sounds like a pretty good catch-all phrase, and I suspect you've heard it before. Seriously, how can *everything* happen for a reason?

Am I really trying to tell you that our paths were somehow prearranged to cross at this very point in our lives? How could that have been done? After all, who can possibly have a reasonable explanation for everything that happens in our personal lives as well as all events around the globe?

Well, there is no doubt this popular expression can be debated with all sorts of points and counterpoints by individuals and intellects with varying perspectives. Can there really be a reason for everything that's going on around us? Can there really be someone in control of everything?

Maybe we're merely floating around, rotating aimlessly on this little planet, and occupying space for a limited period of time. Better yet, who really knows what happens after life on earth? Is there anything afterward? Does anyone know for sure if there is a heaven and hell that last forever?

I'll share with you how I arrived at my conviction that there really is Someone who is directing traffic in the universe, and yes, with absolute indescribable precision and purpose. If you're ready to learn more about this Creator of all that exists, here's a brief introduction:

- He is a supernatural being who is sovereign, all-powerful, all-knowing, omnipresent, perfect, holy, and just.
- He is a Spirit who always was in eternity past, exists currently, and always will be in eternity future.
- He is the one and only true God who created this entire immeasurable universe complete with its countless galaxies, including the Milky Way galaxy where our own solar system resides, all suspended in harmony and total awe.
- He created this unique, extraordinary planet Earth—complete with a perfectly sized moon—and He placed the earth in space at just the right distance away from the sun in order that it will not burn or freeze.
- He created the atmosphere around the earth not only for protection, but also to provide just the right amount of water and oxygen needed for all living things.
- He designed the sun and moon to interact together with the earth and countless other components with

unexplainable accuracy needed to sustain life as we know it to exist.
- He created all living inhabitants of the earth. We (people) are the pinnacle of His design because of the eternal soul He supernaturally breathed into each of us.
- He has an eternal purpose for you and me while we are here on earth, as well as afterward.

In the chapters ahead, I'll share my journey and how I arrived at this point. Yes, everything really does happen for a reason and we were all meant to be here right at this very moment. I was meant to write this book, and you were meant to read it—on purpose by divine intervention.

The supernatural Creator knows us all personally because He designed and wired us in a unique way, while giving us free will. We were all created in His perfect image, but we have strayed from that perfect state. He wants us to do our part and seek Him out, learn about Him, and allow Him into our lives. Ultimately, He wants to grant us access to eternal heaven.

INTRODUCTION

I am a citizen of heaven. Given my limited yet sufficient understanding of what this means, I am immensely humbled and grateful for the privilege to make such a bold statement. My sincere hope is that you will come to the point in your life's journey where you would also gladly apply for citizenship—while the invitation remains available—and know for sure you've received access to heaven. No need to worry about any limits; there is more room available in heaven than anyone can imagine.

The process is simple, yet most people overlook the immeasurable value of this final destination called heaven. The application fee—which no person could afford—has been waived, since the price for admission to heaven had already been 100 percent paid in full. The screening and approval process is instantaneous since the gatekeeper to heaven knows exactly what's in your heart. There is no waiting list. Unfortunately, there aren't many applicants in comparison to the world's population. Best of all, once approved, citizenship into heaven is irrevocable.

In writing and sharing my personal journey with you, I sincerely hope that you too will seek and discover the one and only supernatural Creator of the universe. His desire is that we experience for ourselves His genuine love and grace for humanity at large—for our own good—so that we can rest assured knowing He is in complete control of all things, including access to heaven.

However, arriving at the understanding that the Creator of the universe is in complete control does *not* mean there is unanimous agreement among us humans as to the purpose of life's events as they unfold. It's just not possible for everyone to agree on *why* things happen the way they do. We all see and experience the events in our own lives, as well as the events around us, from our own very limited personal perspective.

Having said that, the fact that there isn't a general agreement on *why* things happen the way they do, does *not* discount or eliminate the possibility that a meaningful purpose for everything really does exist. Without our complete understanding of how the outcome of everything fits into the big picture—due to our mere mortal state—we really have no chance on agreeing on the *why*.

There may have been times in your own life—or perhaps times in the life of someone you know—when you witnessed a miracle, a kind of I-can't-believe-what-just-happened positive-type event.

Someone may have been drowning and his life was saved by a complete stranger who happened to be at the right place at the right time. A game may have been won by a play that defied all odds. A financial resolution may have come out of the blue and prevented major hardship. A terminal tumor or disability may have simply disappeared, much to the surprise of surgeons and family members. Every day, life is conceived and a beautiful baby is born. These are all examples of miracles without complete human understanding. No doubt there are countless others.

Sadly, there are other times when the expression *how can this happen* or *this is just not fair* comes to mind. These are a sort of I-can't-believe-the-terrible-thing-that-just-happened negative-type event.

A tsunami may have resulted in mass devastation to a coastal population someplace in the world. Radioactive mishaps may have caused extensive damage to nearby communities. Mass shootings for no apparent reason may have created sheer chaos. Charismatic leaders and dictators with ill intent may have taken over, abused, and destroyed entire villages. Earthquakes, tornados, hurricanes, avalanches, and wildfires can all be relentless and merciless to life.

Car accidents can snuff out someone's life without warning, even if that someone wasn't at fault.

These are all examples of what we would consider negative-type events. They are difficult to process but even more difficult to rationalize in our minds. We think, *What good reason can there possibly be for these kinds of devastating events?*

If you were to approach the Creator of the universe with a humble heart, especially when you don't understand the purpose or reasons for tragic events, you would embark on the journey leading you in the right direction toward citizenship to heaven. I encourage you to take the first step toward the Creator. Sincerely ask Him to reveal Himself and help you to get to know Him. He's always within your reach. All you need to do is crack open the door of your heart and begin listening to what He has to say. Besides inner peace and comfort, you have *forever* to gain.

1
UNHIDDEN AGENDA

*And we know that all things work together
for good to those who love God,
to those who are the called according to His purpose.*
—Romans 8:28

The idea of writing a book started about seventeen years ago for me, shortly after my first marriage ended abruptly in the year 2000. I couldn't make any sense of it. I felt betrayed and lied to. *What a waste,* I thought. *This was not supposed to happen. What about the kids?* I didn't sleep much during that time, instead reflecting on the bizarre events taking place right before my very eyes, and doing my best to try and clear the dense fog I seemed to be trapped in.

After about six months, I realized the sun still came up every morning. This seemingly simple event was sufficient reassurance that God was still in control, so I made the decision to begin moving forward again, trusting that everything would somehow turn out okay. In retrospect, I am more grateful for every one of those strange events than I can express in a few paragraphs.

As the truth began to surface, I recall telling others somewhat jokingly, "Someday I'm going to write a book." Although I said those words more than just a few times, the mere thought of writing a couple of chapters was not something I looked forward to doing. For a long time, I continued to steer as far away as possible from the subject of writing. I recall encouraging my son Kyle to write instead; he's truly the one with exceptional natural writing talent, even confirmed by an expert playwright and author we went to see.

Maybe that was it. Maybe I'd brought this onto myself while trying to advise my son to write. It's all good, as it was likely meant to be this way.

I tried my best not to think about writing, but the day came when I could no longer continue to ignore it. It gnawed at me from the inside, and I knew I needed to start writing. I was convinced I had the message in my heart for a reason. What I had to say was important, and I needed to figure out a way to express it on paper. At the very least, I was hoping the words I was compelled to write would not only spark conversations among people from all walks of life, but would also empower my readers to ultimately make an informed personal decision when faced with the critical choice between Creation and Evolution. Your personal reference and absolute conviction toward how everything all around us came into existence from the very beginning is of immense importance.

It's been said that when starting a painting using a blank canvas, the most difficult line to draw is the first one. I can attest that the same can be said of the first words that were needed when starting to write on a blank computer screen. After putting aside all the excuses, I felt a sense of responsibility to document my thoughts, so I was compelled to begin by writing bits and pieces, then a table of contents unfolded for some structure.

It seemed to take a while at first, but I finally started to believe this assignment was worthy of both my time and energy. More importantly, due to the very nature of the subject having eternal consequences, I wanted to organize my thoughts and message in a straight-forward, common-sense way. I didn't want to get all tangled up in hypothetical theories. I wanted everything to be conveyed in an easy-to-understand manner. I made a commitment to embark on this journey with simplicity, compassion, persistence, and patience, while trusting that the right message would come across on the pages.

I've asked myself numerous times whether writing this book would make any difference in the grand scheme of things. Needling questions abounded: Would it really matter in any meaningful way to anyone? Why would I take on such an endeavor, and who am I doing this for anyway? I mean, I'm just a regular guy with a grateful story I'd like to share. How would I even begin to sort through everything I wanted to say?

Admittedly, I encountered self-doubt many times as I watched the deadlines I had occasionally set for myself pass by, one after another. Honestly, as time rolled forward, the bottled-up message seemed to grow more uncomfortable, so I kept adding a few paragraphs here and there to relieve the pressure. For some reason, I felt compelled to keep inching forward, one thought, one sentence, and one paragraph at a time.

I will also readily admit that I tend to reflect a lot more nowadays than during my younger, more foolish years. Perhaps it's because I'm a parent. Perhaps it's because events in my life unfolded the way they did. Or perhaps it's because I believe I have a message of unfathomable importance to spread to others.

The subjects of creation, evolution, heaven, and hell are extremely deep subjects, with personal and often divisive opinions. Disagreements on these subjects can quickly escalate, and people can become resentful. Where would I even begin, and more importantly, what new argument could I possibly make? Would I be able to convey this message with clarity, and how would I go about doing so? What I was struggling with most was whether this book would really help anyone.

One day I simply decided to write, and I began the journey of organizing my thoughts and putting things down without reservation and without knowing how it would all unfold. Sometimes months would go by without a single paragraph written. I would jot down ideas found in articles and other research to be expanded at some point. Yes, it's taken me a while, but I kept at it. Moving forward with each written sentence, I found that the purpose for continuing became clearer. I knew in my heart that I had to do this. I remember thinking, *If only one person benefits from reading this, then my effort will certainly have been worth it.*

It all boiled down to choosing to write with the hope to inspire someone to seek citizenship in heaven. That was it. My unhidden agenda was to help someone. That was the thought I kept front and center, motivating me to complete this book.

Reflection Questions

Who is important in your life?

_____
_____
_____
_____
_____
_____
_____
_____
_____
_____
_____
_____

Do you realize that God has a purpose for you?

_____
_____
_____
_____
_____
_____
_____
_____
_____
_____
_____
_____

2

RODICA

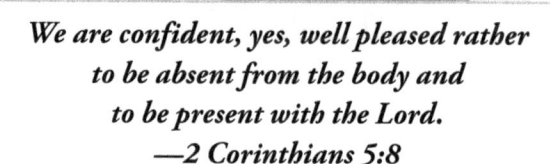

*We are confident, yes, well pleased rather
to be absent from the body and
to be present with the Lord.*
—*2 Corinthians 5:8*

By all accounts, I shouldn't have survived. I have never shied away from talking about the accident with anyone who wanted to know what I saw, heard, and felt that night. I'm honored to share my younger sister's story and mine with anyone who asks. I didn't realize it at the time, but I now have no doubt that I survived because of a bigger purpose behind it all. This single event that took place over thirty-six years ago had an immense impact on how I viewed life from that day forward.

The scene of the accident was nothing short of horrific. My sister had been driving the car while I slept across the backseat. According to the police report, our car was traveling at about sixty miles per hour going northbound on I-15 in Nevada, when for no apparent reason, the car began to drift from the right lane onto the nearby paved shoulder, which offered no warning of a different sound. The car continued drifting to the right, then all four wheels hopped the raised curb that separated the highway from the desert landscape. After traveling on the desert surface for another 471 feet, the tire tracks indicated an attempt had been made to get the car back onto the highway. This is where the accident turned fatal.

The raised curb, from the desert side, posed a higher obstacle to overcome as the vehicle was speeding back toward the highway lanes. The car's front left tire got caught on the curb, which drove deep gouge marks into the rim, and couldn't negotiate the higher curb surface. The momentum of the vehicle trying to veer to the left caused the car to flip end over end. It landed on the driver's-side roof, then rolled over three times, according to the witness driving behind us, before finally careening to a stop in the middle of the two-lane highway, facing the wrong way.

When I regained consciousness, I heard the screeching of tires from other cars coming toward us. Miraculously, no other vehicle got tangled up with ours. I then sat up in the back seat, looked around, and realized that my sister wasn't in the car. At first, I thought I was dreaming; I looked everywhere, trying to register what I was seeing, but the realization that something terrible had just happened was sinking in quickly. By this time, other vehicles had stopped on the highway with their headlights pointing our way. I looked around again, then pushed the front seat up so I could get out of the two-door vehicle and look for her.

After stepping on the broken glass on the floor as I got out, I walked around the car and found my sister lying on the pavement about six feet from the driver's door. She wasn't moving or breathing when I knelt beside her. I recall holding her head, then giving her a couple of breaths of air; adrenaline was flowing through my body. She had sustained fatal injuries, and it became obvious to me by what I saw and felt holding her. I remember thinking that I was glad she didn't suffer. I kept holding her, not wanting to believe what had just happened.

My sister's name was Rodica. She was only eighteen years old, three years younger than I, and God had just taken her soul to eternal heaven.

This all took place on a Saturday evening, just after ten p.m. on December 27, 1980. A friend of ours was in the front passenger seat, and he sustained a broken bone to his left foot. Miraculously, I only had a few minor bruises and scratches.

Rodica was beautiful, smart, kind, courageous, and, most importantly, had a purified heart. Although her life on earth was brief, she left a positive impact on people's lives everywhere she went. Very good friends, we had shared our hopes, dreams, and even fears on many occasions.

For some time immediately following the accident, I wondered why it had to happen. I could not make any sense of it. Looking for answers, I continually recounted the day's events. Many circumstances had brought us all to that horrific moment in time, but I was always comforted beyond explanation by knowing that she was in heaven. Three years earlier, Rodica had learned enough about God that she decided to be obedient to biblical teaching, being baptized and confessing publicly her faith and trust in God's Son Jesus.

Although I didn't understand why God needed to take her from this earth at such a young age, I knew He held all the answers and that I needed to trust Him going forward. The thought *Why did I survive?* crossed my mind many times over the years. Why did our friend survive as well? Although I have grieved the loss of my sister, I have never blamed anyone for what had happened. It was no one's fault. I truly believe that God saw it as being appropriate for this to happen exactly the way it unfolded. Looking back, I have no doubt that God had additional plans for my life, so my time wasn't up that day.

So here is that expression again: *Everything happens for a reason.*

Whether we understand the events around us or not is irrelevant. Whether we agree with the events or not is also irrelevant. Knowing that everything happens with God's complete knowledge, understanding, and permission is *very* relevant. What I know for sure is that I need to humble myself before God and trust Him daily, for my own good. He has known the future from the very beginning.

I am a walking miracle having survived the accident, which had an indescribable impact on my life. It's been on my heart to share my story with you at this moment. You are reading this because you were meant to. Perhaps it's an invitation for you to humble your heart as well, and appreciate this gift of life you have. Perhaps it's a reminder for you to seek out the God of the Bible for yourself so you also can rest assured that He's in control of everything around us all.

Life is precious, but it can be brief. You can lose it in the blink of an eye when it's least expected. Knowing God, the Creator of the universe, and being right with Him matters more than you can imagine. Having the assurance of citizenship in heaven, which God alone can grant, while here on earth will bring you inner peace, even when you don't understand all of life's events. Best of all, with God in your heart, you can be a blessing to someone else during a time when they need it most.

Reflection Questions

Was there an event that happened in your life where you couldn't explain why it had to be that way?

_____
_____
_____
_____
_____
_____
_____

Did you come to terms with it and accept it anyway?

_____
_____
_____
_____
_____
_____
_____

Is there someone close to you who passed away unexpectedly? Did that person know God?

_____
_____
_____
_____
_____
_____
_____

3

BACKGROUNDS, PIT STOPS, DETOURS, AND DESTINATIONS

Enter through the narrow gate. For wide is the gate and broad is the road that leads to destruction, and many enter through it. But small is the gate and narrow the road that leads to life, and only a few find it.
—Matthew 7:13–14 NIV

Our ancestors originated in various nations and parts of the world with different backgrounds and traditions. That means we're all unique. Based on our past exposure as well as current events in our lives, we're able to generate individual ideas and opinions about what we see, hear, and feel about every facet of our existence and what's happening all around us.

As unique as we may all be on the outside, there are many more things we have in common, if we were to look on the inside. We all have red blood running through our veins, sustaining life in our bodies. We all have feelings, a conscience, and the need to belong and be loved. We also intuitively know right from wrong.

We have the ability to discern when an injustice has been done. Most importantly, we all have an intricate brain to help us think independently. We have the capability of observing, gathering, sorting, evaluating, and reasoning all sorts of information on virtually an infinite number of topics, regardless of the source. We then have the choice to keep those things we consider valid and true, while dismissing those things that are fake and false.

We have the ability and freedom to choose our thoughts, the words we speak, and the actions we take. If we could stop long enough to look through our mind's eye (or see from a higher perspective far above the earth's surface), we would find that there are more important similar things that are common among all people on earth than there are differences. For example, we're all someone's son or daughter, someone's husband or wife, someone's father or mother, someone's colleague, or someone's friend. We may also be an employee or an entrepreneur, an athlete ... or an author.

Our individual backgrounds, the temporary places we've visited, the short pit stops we've made, the people we've been in contact with, and all the information we've gathered throughout our lives will no doubt influence the final destination of each of us. On the surface, this subject of final destination in life seems like it should involve simplicity and common sense, but nothing can be further from the truth.

A bit about me and my background: I was born in Bucharest, Romania. When I was eleven years old, my dad, my older brother, and I arrived in Montreal, Quebec, as legal landed immigrants. It was mid-January of 1971, and we had flown into Canada after spending the prior six months in West Germany, Austria, and Hungary. Our trip had started in early summer of 1970, when the three of us left Romania for vacation.

As I understood it at the time, my mom and my two sisters, one older and one younger, could not come with us because they were not granted travel visas. The Romanian government at the time tended to keep half the family in the country, with the unspoken intention that the other half of the family would return home after vacation was over. We had visas to go through Hungary, enter Czechoslovakia, and then return home the same way.

As it turned out, my dad took a detour from Hungary and we headed for Austria. I recall my dad telling my brother and I that we might be turned away at the Austrian border since we had no valid visa to enter but it was worth a try. My dad had been to Austria before with my mom, so he had an idea of what the country was about. It was a free country, which was what my dad wanted for his entire family. His vision was to have us all free from the suppression of the communist system that ruled Romania.

As we approached the Austrian border, we stopped and then watched as the officer leafed through the pages of my dad's passport. He said something to us in German, but we just shrugged and shook our heads, not understanding even a word. He stared at the expired stamped visas on the pages of the passport with a confused look on his face, then eyed each of us one last time, appearing to debate what to do. Then he handed the passport back to my dad and motioned for us to proceed. We were free to enter the country.

That was it.

Within three minutes, we were in Austria. My dad, although happy and relieved, celebrated quietly, knowing that we were now in a free country. Our first stop was at a convenience store where he bought us some chewing gum. Now my brother and I were celebrating; chewing gum wasn't available in Romania at the time.

"We're not going back, but we're going to bring your mom and sisters to be with us here," my dad told us. In the next few days, he eventually was able to contact my mom with the news. The plan was for my mom and my sisters to go to the Romanian authorities and apply for visas to join us in Austria.

The process, as it turned out, was not so simple. My mom was rejected countless times, falsely accused by the Romanian authorities of knowing about my father's escape plan. I can only imagine the fear of uncertainty and sleepless nights both my parents endured. We were in touch with her occasionally to find out how things were proceeding, but all we could do was encourage her to keep trying.

The three of us slept in our car, a Renault 10, for a few nights since funds were limited. Somehow we arrived at a sort of government-sponsored camp in Austria where landed immigrants were given a place to stay temporarily, and my dad had a chance to find work. He was an experienced tailor, and even though he didn't speak the language, he found work without much difficulty. Over the next few weeks, things seemed to settle down a bit, or at least it seemed that way to me.

By early fall of 1970, it had become clear to my dad that if we were to remain in Europe, we would likely never be reunited with the other half of our family. Austria was too close to Romania, he thought. It seemed like a chess match as to who would give in first. Would my dad decide to return, risking the possibility of jail or worse, or would the Romanian authorities issue visas to my mom and sisters?

Based on outside advice, my father made the decision we needed to go to either the United States or Canada. We hoped that once there, the Romanian authorities would finally grant the women in our family the visas they needed. Once across the ocean on a different continent, we counted on a positive outcome and a quick family reunion. We needed to go through West Germany, where visas to North America were being granted.

The gated camp for landed immigrants in West Germany was similar to the one in Austria. My brother and I attended a school set up at the camp specifically for kids of many nations. We met and played with other foreign kids, while learning to speak German. As fall turned into winter, I recall my dad waking me on a few cold mornings because the car wouldn't start and he needed to get to work. Still in our pajamas, my brother and I would push-start the manual-transmission four-speed Renault. My dad popped the clutch to get the engine started, then drove away while waving at us. Ah, the memories!

My dad chose Canada instead of the United States, primarily due to the uncertainties of the potential draft and the unresolved Vietnam War. The three of us left West Germany and landed in Montreal, Quebec, in mid-January of 1971. It was very cold, and we didn't know anyone. We didn't speak any English and only knew a bit of French. After my dad made a few phone calls to complete strangers picked from a phone book—people with Romanian-sounding last names—we ended up on a train heading to London, Ontario, then to Windsor a week or so later.

While in a class to learn English, my dad met the pastor of the Romanian Baptist church in Windsor. We were befriended with the pastor's family as well as others in the congregation, and began to attend services. My brother and I learned to play mandolin after joining in the church orchestra.

I was eleven years old and my brother was about fourteen. Soon, everyone at the church knew that my mom and two sisters were still back in Romania. A lot of people were praying for the reunion of our family. The pastor's wife would invite us over for Sunday lunches, and during a conversation with her one day, she advised me that it would help if I asked God to help my mom and sisters get the visas they needed. She told me that God knew our situation and would hear me, even though I didn't fully understand how this would happen.

About a year went by without any glimmer of hope for my mom and sisters. Perhaps out of despair, my dad decided that we should go back to Europe. We ended up selling our few belongings and flew to France. He reasoned that perhaps being back in

Europe would bring about the change our family was hoping for. As I recall, we now encountered a different problem. We were no longer allowed immigration status in Europe since we had already accepted Canada from our previous visit. Suffice it to say, we flew back to Canada.

While lying in bed one night, I stared up at the ceiling and said, "God, if you're really there, if you truly exist, if you can really hear me, and if you know our situation, then please help my mom and sisters be able to leave Romania to join us in Canada." I had no idea anyone was listening, but I figured it couldn't hurt to try.

The pastor's wife was right. She had encouraged me to talk to God and assured me that He would listen, and I will forever be grateful for her advice. Shortly thereafter, my mom and my sisters were finally granted visas.

In June of 1972, after about two years apart, our family was reunited. We were together in a free country.

My mom is a very strong woman. During the prior two years, even though we did our best to be as supportive as we could, my mom managed to singlehandedly overcome obstacles and adversities that I cannot even imagine. In spite of numerous difficulties and sleepless nights, and seemingly against all odds with the Romanian authorities, she moved forward, believing that eventually she would see us again. I learned later that she prayed constantly, as did my grandparents who were all back home as well.

My dad is a quiet, hardworking man who minds his own business and continuously looks for ways to improve, and I have no doubt that he strived for a better life for his entire family. We came to North America, reaping all the associated blessings of being in a free country. I will always give him credit for his effort to bring his family out of a suppressive society and provide us an opportunity for a brighter future. Still, it sometimes felt like we were all being tossed by the wind as we made our way through Europe, then Canada. The disagreements between my parents continued even after the reunion, and sadly the ultimate cost was a split family as of mid-1975.

I've always appreciated the sacrifices both my parents made for us kids. Their work ethic is second to none, and that has rubbed off on us. To suggest that our family's road to North America was difficult would be an understatement. Very few things that are worthwhile are easy. I'm thankful beyond words for both my parents. They have my utmost respect, and I love them with all my heart.

Fast forward a few years. My older brother and sister married their spouses, then in December 1980, my younger sister and I were involved in that fateful car accident. In 1984 I married my first wife, and we had my son and three daughters. Respect, appreciation, and excellent character were some of the topics I talked to my kids about regularly. They remind me to this day that some of those early conversations also included the importance of cash flow and leverage. I actually don't mind these reminders at all.

I've come to learn, accept, and appreciate that everything really *does* happen for a reason, regardless of whether or not I understand it.

Much to my surprise, my marriage dissolved in the year 2000. I actually thought the world was coming to an end, as I also witnessed the tragedy of September 11, 2001 on live TV with the rest of the world. Although heartbroken for my kids, I knew they were meant to be born into this world. I somehow knew they would be okay. They are all unique, talented, and kindhearted, and my life has been enriched by each of them. I love them and care deeply about their well-being, and I've done my best to let them know that through my words and actions.

In the summer of 2006, I remarried. It was nothing short of divine intervention, and I've been so grateful for yet another miracle. I love my wife, Tracey, more than words can express. She is bright, beautiful, creative, adventurous, kind, supportive, and, best of all, she loves God. I've been blessed with an immediate family who has been on my side without judgment, regardless of what was happening in my life. It's during the difficult times that you learn the most about yourself and the character of those around you. I am fortunate and blessed.

I've tried to summarize some of my background, pit stops, and detours, as well as my current destination, to give you a better idea of where I've come from. We each have our own personal life journey, and I say embrace it, even though you don't know the future.

What's been truly liberating for me recently is that I've learned to not allow the things that I can do nothing about get under my skin. I'm not suggesting that's easy; I'm learning to bring those things to God instead. I do my best every day to trust in the Creator of the universe, seeking His guidance and knowing that it's for my best interest.

So if someone is spreading lies or rumors and you know what the truth is, keep your inner peace because the truth is all that matters. We all love our kids, our immediate and extended families, friends, coworkers, neighbors, and others. Ultimately, I'm getting better at realizing that my kids have grown up and are mature enough to make decisions for themselves. Even though I've made many mistakes over the years, I'm thankful that I only have a few true regrets.

It's extremely important to point out that where I am today, and where you are today, is not our final destination. Our current place in life is only a pit stop. It's been said many times that life is short. Whether someone passes away from this life before birth, as an infant or child, or at age forty, sixty, eighty, or one hundred, that person's soul will end up in one of two final destinations forever—a place of eternal bliss or a place of eternal torment.

Ultimately, if you're mature enough to acknowledge there is a God, then know for sure that your final eternal destination, heaven or hell, will also depend on your belief in Him. Your understanding of who the Creator of the entire universe is, your relationship with Him on a regular basis, and the choices and decisions you've made throughout your life will no doubt affect your destiny. My hope and prayer is that you seek out this supernatural Creator and humble yourself while you have the opportunity. Nothing can possibly be more important for your everlasting well-being.

Forever is a *very* long time.

Reflection Questions

Do you believe there is a heaven and hell?
_____
_____
_____
_____
_____
_____
_____
_____

Do you know for sure if you have God's assurance for access to heaven as your final destination?
_____
_____
_____
_____
_____
_____
_____
_____

Have you spoken to Him lately?
_____
_____
_____
_____
_____
_____
_____
_____

4
QUESTIONS

*Blessed are those who find wisdom,
those who gain understanding.*
—Proverbs 3:13 NIV

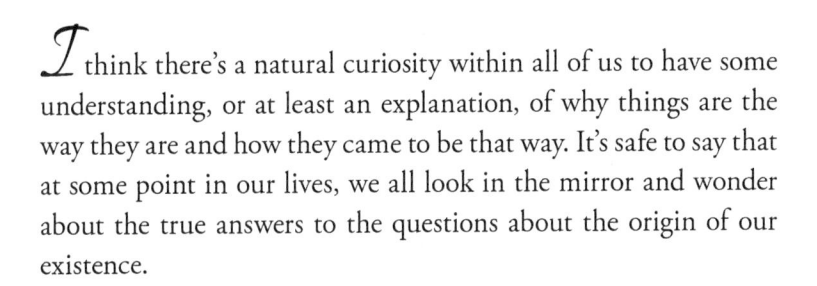

$\mathcal{I}$ think there's a natural curiosity within all of us to have some understanding, or at least an explanation, of why things are the way they are and how they came to be that way. It's safe to say that at some point in our lives, we all look in the mirror and wonder about the true answers to the questions about the origin of our existence.

- Where did we—people, animals, every living thing on earth—come from?
- How and when did we get here?
- Why is the design of this planet that we all live on so special that it can sustain life while floating around in the vastness of space among countless other planets and galaxies?

- How long has the entire universe been around, and how did it come into existence?
- Can the earth continue to survive floating among countless gigantic moving objects through space?
- Can life on earth be indefinite, given all the existing circumstances and activities going on?
- What would the future of the universe look like, and should we even care?
- Why are we even here?
- What happens after we die?

Regardless of anyone's personal views, opinions, or theories, these questions cannot be avoided by any rational person, even if they try not to think about them. From the very early stages of life—whether taught by our parents or other family members, learned within the education system, influenced through conversation within our inner circle of friends and acquaintances, or perhaps from history books or other documents—we all formulate individual opinions regarding these very profound yet common-sense questions.

Right or wrong, most people tend to quickly dismiss these topics because they're not easy to understand. This, however, is the very reason these topics are so important. However, we can all rationalize and agree that this earth and all life on it had a beginning. As well, if we're asked to explain how life began, it is safe to say our minds get stretched to their limits. No human being can even begin to generate completely satisfying answers acceptable to every skeptic. The very different individual beliefs generated as being true and the acceptable answers to the start and meaning of life often cause frustration or provoke controversy, unrest, and even war.

Let's for a minute take a different approach.

Have you ever wondered what you can really achieve in life? Even if you were able to quickly accumulate, through honest work, a comfortable standard of living, would you then think that you have reached your potential and consider yourself set for life? Would you be satisfied with your accomplishments, or would you continue to accumulate more of everything? At some point, you may begin to reason that you have earned, and possibly even justify that you deserve, the very best life has to offer as a reward for your years of steadfast labor, dedication, persistence, or outright wit. You have outsmarted most everyone at the game of life. Eat, drink, and be merry! Life is good!

On the other hand, success may not come your way as easily as you thought it would during your younger days. You may constantly find yourself having to deal with unexpected twists and turns and obstacles that pop up, leaving you feeling like you're on the treadmill of life going nowhere fast. You know you're putting in lots of effort, but with little noticeable progress. Sometimes things just aren't coming together as you'd like.

You do your very best to plan your next steps, but surprises continue to impede the progress you envisioned. Nevertheless, you pick up the pieces, dig your heels in, dust yourself off, and press forward, hoping for a better tomorrow. It may not happen until later in life, but with persistence, you finally arrive in the place where you conclude you have everything you need.

As time passes, you may even try to convince yourself that you couldn't possibly run out of resources for as long as you live on this earth. Your thoughts may focus on your current age. You quickly consider the average life expectancy, then sit back, look around, and conclude that you have years of celebration on easy street ahead of you. Yet faint, persistent inner voices and feelings tell you that something's missing, then take up residence deep down within the core of your being.

During the quiet moments of your thought life, you may not want to admit what's happening, because you can't really say for sure why these voices and feelings are even there. What could possibly be missing? After all, you have everything you need. You do your best to ignore them, but your conscience is hard at work, constantly wrestling with the reality of thoughts about the end of life. What happens after death seems to migrate to the front burner of your mind with the passage of time.

Life continues to move forward, and you still may not be able to elaborate on this inner anxiety that grows stronger with time. You may even try to convince yourself there is really nothing to be concerned about. Even though you have accumulated everything you can possibly need, the realization of your temporary existence as a mortal being sets in and you need to face it.

Many people may not want to admit this, but the source of their inner discomfort stems from simply being unsure of what happens in the afterlife. What *really* happens after you die? Most people, being totally honest about the subject, will admit that a certain something has been missing. They are simply not sure if anything exists on the other side.

Is there really a place of bliss and a place of torment after life on earth ends? And if such places do exist, then how good do you have to be in order to land in the place of bliss and avoid the place of torment? You may try to reason that perhaps there really aren't such places; they're simply a hoax. On the other hand, you might ask yourself, *What if these places turn out to be for real after all? If so, where will I end up?*

You silently struggle with your answers because you reason that there's no way of knowing for sure. After all, you're still alive but you suspect that you will only have one chance to get this right. So what do you do? Where do you turn for answers? How will you know which of the answers you come across will be true and which will be false? Who will you trust to guide you in the right direction? Will you have the courage to be honest with yourself and share what you have learned with loved ones in your life?

The answers to these questions are difficult. At some point, most people come face-to-face with these uncertainties. We're all mortals. More often than not, if faced with the question of the existence of some sort of afterlife, most people will say they can only *hope* to end up in a place with no pain, or in a place of peace with honor and dignity.

If we're honest with ourselves, we all want to have control of our present situation and our future. We can generally reason that little can be done about our past except to learn from the experiences and move on. Many people will also conclude that they can control some things about their present situation, and that choosing certain actions will favorably impact their lives.

However, when it comes to considering future destination possibilities for life after death, most people will admit feelings of uncertainty, concern, anxiety, and possibly even fear. They don't know for sure where they'll end up. They have no conviction. The concerns about the immediate future as well as the mystery of what happens after life on earth ends are the subjects of many debates, and there is certainly no shortage of opinions and beliefs.

The main focus and intent of the chapters ahead is to point out in very simple terms that each person's views about what the future looks like is totally dependent on their personal answer to the question, *How did it all start?* It seems to all come down to this basic yet critical choice: creation or evolution? We are all faced with making this choice at some point in our lives. The argument is that a person can't possibly know where their final destination may be if they're not convinced in their soul of how it all began in the first place.

Did this earth, and life on earth, evolve by mere chance, or was everything supernaturally created by God at a specific point in time for a specific purpose? Or did the world and life as we know it simply come from a "big bang"? If each person's views about the future are founded on their personal belief regarding the beginning of everything, then it would seem reasonable that each person be well advised to take the time, and put in the effort needed, to investigate and examine the facts about the beginning, for themselves, before making this most-critical choice.

Reflection Questions

What questions do you have about how life began in the universe?

_____
_____
_____
_____
_____
_____
_____
_____

What steps have you taken to gain understanding and wisdom on this topic?

_____
_____
_____
_____
_____
_____
_____

Who will you trust as being the authority on this subject?

_____
_____
_____
_____
_____
_____
_____
_____

5

CREATION OR EVOLUTION? ONLY ONE CAN BE TRUE

For since the creation of the world, God's invisible qualities, His eternal power and divine nature, have been clearly seen, being understood from His workmanship, so that men are without excuse.
—Romans 1:20 BSB

Choices, choices, and more choices. They're everywhere, part of everyday life. You can't get away from making choices on an ongoing basis, no matter how hard you try.

According to *Webster's Revised Unabridged Dictionary*, the word *choice* can be described as "an act of choosing; the voluntary act of selecting or separating from two or more things that which is preferred; the determination of the mind in preferring one thing to another."[1]

Notice that the act of choosing is a voluntary act of selection. Also notice that Webster described it as a "determination of the

---

[1] *Webster's Revised Unabridged Dictionary*, s.v. "choice," *Biblehub*, accessed January 22, 2018, http://biblehub.com/topical/c/choice.htm.

mind." It would be safe to conclude that your brain is able to make these distinct, preferred determinations based on the information it has retained. Our minds are like computers designed to give us signals that convince us to perform the act of choosing in such a way that is most beneficial or "preferred."

Past civilizations have asked many times:

- Did everything we see around us evolve over a long period of time, or is there a divine Creator who spoke everything into existence at a specific point in time?
- What was the cause of all that can be seen, as well as all the forces that cannot be seen?
- What brought everything into existence?
- What continues to sustain everything?

We currently have more intelligence on these subjects than was available hundreds of years ago. We believe we can see everything that exists and can rely on experimentation, DNA sampling, common sense, and logic. We should be able to reason and somehow agree on particular answers.

Unfortunately, people across the globe are completely divided and cannot agree on common answers to these questions. Was all life a result of evolution, creation, or something else still unknown? Ignoring the subject altogether is also a possible scenario, but that in itself can also be considered a choice.

It's probably safe to say that the answer people choose to the question, "How did life begin?" will shape the path of their life. With infinite importance, I daresay that the answer chosen by an individual—either creation or evolution—will also bring about personal consequences that are eternal in nature. When it comes to this critical question, we must become informed through research, and choose wisely. All of us will be held individually accountable for the choice we make.

From the moment we were born, our brains were pre-programmed with information that causes involuntary actions, such as our lungs breathing and our heart pumping blood throughout the body so that life can exist. Our eyes, ears, nose, fingers, toes, and numerous complex internal organs are all working as they were purposefully intended, in order to sustain life. As a baby is nourished and grows older, a unique personality blossoms. Over the next few years, a vast amount of information continues to be absorbed by the young mind, like a dry sponge absorbing water when submerged.

The result is that both the source as well as the content of the information being absorbed by the developing mind will shape the individual's voluntary act of choice. What is also interesting is that the manner in which the information is presented also has a great impact on how much of the information is retained.

While these are mere observations, there is no dispute about the pre-programmed information that exists within the mind of every newborn. Then additional information is gathered in the mind, and that is ultimately tapped into for making voluntary choices later in life, based on that foundation.

This may sound like common sense. As the expression goes, *garbage in, garbage out.* We are all pre-wired in a way to be self-sustaining with the ability to add information, thus increasing our capacity to understand and discern good from bad, right from wrong. We think, *Is the information valid or invalid? Should I store this information because it's true, or dismiss it because it's false?*

Within these short years lived on earth, we all get to choose the type of information we retain as valid input to our onboard computer. The output or our reaction to various events that happen around us will depend on our individual conviction of the quality and validity of the input information we've stored over time.

If a person voluntarily makes a choice or a decision about any one thing over another, that person will either benefit from it or suffer negative consequences. The main point here is that before choosing, the responsibility is with the individual to carefully consider and evaluate the facts presented.

———∞∞◦❦◦∞∞———

Recent research tells us that the average adult in the United States makes about 35,000 decisions every day[2], most of which are pretty basic: toast, eggs, red shirt, dark shoes, open door, close door, walk, run, sit, start car, stop at red light, look, listen, talk, read, work, rest, eat, drink, bike ride, movie, dinner, and more. One can see how these decisions can add up pretty quickly throughout the day. Decisions just happen, and we often take them for granted.

At first glance, many decisions we make are automatic; we don't need to think about them because they are instinctive to our survival. Most of the decisions we make on a daily basis have to do with the necessities of life: health, food, shelter, and clothing. Other decisions are influenced by our financial means and are not necessarily our preferences. What can we afford to buy at that moment? What kind of dining room set will be practical yet also fit the budget? Which car or truck do we need or like? How big of a house or apartment should we live in? Our age, family, health, and a host of other factors play a huge role in how we make decisions.

However, it seems that life in general gets more complex with every passing decade, as people are faced with more choices and decisions. Perhaps life can even become fuzzy at times, given all the options we're faced with every day. More choices are not necessarily a bad thing; they're simply more things to consider, juggle, evaluate, and process.

In addition, we're also bombarded with a variety of advertisements from every possible angle. Various companies cater

---

[2] Dr. Joel Hoomans, "35,000 Decisions: The Great Choices of Strategic Leaders," *Roberts Wesleyan College*, March 20, 2015, accessed January 22, 2018, https://go.roberts.edu/leadingedge/the-great-choices-of-strategic-leaders.

to our human senses, all trying to attract us and influence our decisions to choose one item over another. Hundreds of millions of dollars are spent continuously in studies on human thought patterns, preferences, behaviors, habits, fads, and fashions. They're all designed with the sole purpose of having individuals choose one item over another. All kinds of follow-up satisfaction surveys and psychological studies become reports showing how to influence our decisions. The ultimate goal is to improve a company's financial bottom line.

Regardless of where we live on this planet, and irrespective of the condition or our individual status within society, we all exercise the freedom of choice. This happens every moment of every day, whether we realize it or not.

- Wake up early or sleep in?
- Exercise in the morning, later in the evening, or not at all?
- Meet up with friends now or later?
- Schedule activities or do nothing and simply allow events to unfold?
- Vote for candidate one, candidate two, or neither of them?
- Save more of what I earn or spend everything I earn?
- Have pizza or wings for dinner?
- Seek more answers or accept popular belief?

We can even choose to build or destroy, empower or suppress, encourage or ridicule, love or hate, enrich or hurt, move forward or remain stagnant. Being exposed to countless choices and decisions every day, we face one unique choice that is very different from all the others—and of utmost importance. The validity of the foundation of stored input required to make this choice cannot be more critical.

How did it all start? Was it mere-coincidence evolution, or was it supernaturally designed creation by God Himself? What will you choose as your response? What input of information have you stored that you can count on as being true or valid to lead you to the right answer? Everything you experience in life, as well as your final eternal destination, will be shaped by the choice you make. What can possibly be more important?

We can all respect each other's individual backgrounds, opinions, and personal beliefs, but at the very heart of it, we cannot all be right when it comes to the subject of origins. How it all started can only have one correct answer. Logically, there can only be one way it all began. That "beginning" has unfolded into what we all see today, in a very unique way.

When contemplating the size of the universe, our imaginations are quickly stretched to the limits of what we can conceive and understand. It's a matter of what we know exists, starting with the immeasurable vast universe that spans countless light years in distance, complete with innumerable galaxies, down to our very own Milky Way containing gazillions of other stars, down to our very own solar system within the Milky Way, and finally zooming in to our unique, life-sustaining planet Earth. Did this all evolve, or was it supernaturally created? It takes faith to believe either, but only one can be true.

Let's pretend for a moment there is a multiple-choice test that all humans are required to take. This test has one question: *How did the universe, with all its galaxies, stars, planets, and inhabitants of earth, come into existence?* There are only two choices offered. Certainly, there would not be 100 percent agreement.

We know there are different opinions and beliefs about how it all began, so the test results would essentially prove nothing. The key point here is that even if all people on earth took the test, and everyone respected everyone else's choice, it simply doesn't matter. Respecting each other's opinions on the subject of creation and evolution has nothing to do with the validity of the true nature of one and the false nature of the other.

There can only be one answer that is true and valid for the beginning of everything. It's safe to say there was a specific way in which it all came to be. As well, a general statement can be made that we all want to know the truth ... about anything. No matter what circumstances you may find yourself in; no matter the reasons for how you got into those circumstances; no matter what person you may be talking with or seeking advice from; no matter what book you may be looking for answers in; no matter the influences of your life experiences, your education, or your upbringing; no matter what your parents', siblings', or friends' beliefs may be; no matter your skin color; no matter if you're rich or poor; and no matter where you live—inevitably one day you will find yourself all alone with only your thoughts about this. You will be searching in the depths of your soul for the truth.

We all long to know the truth of how we came into existence while also wondering what, if anything, may come after this life has ended. You somehow know down deep inside that you're the only one who will be accountable for the choice you've made between creation and evolution. At some point in your life, your conscience will put you in a position to choose. You may consider putting it off, or you may tell yourself there is no decision to be made because you have lots of time. Either way, you're actually making a choice to delay the inevitable or simply choosing neither.

Every one of us—either consciously or subconsciously—makes a choice on the subject of creation or evolution, whether we admit it or not. Both options require faith. Only *one* can possibly be true. We're all mere mortals, and ultimately we each make our own decision while here on earth. After we take our final breath, our eternal destination will depend to a large degree on where we each stood on this subject. I encourage you to research the topic for yourself. There isn't anything of greater importance, as one path leads to eternal bliss while the other leads to eternal turmoil.

Reflection Questions

Are you not in total awe when you look out and see how our planet Earth is maintaining life in such amazing balance within the vastness of space?

_____
_____
_____
_____
_____
_____
_____
_____
_____
_____
_____

Do you believe this came to be this way by perfect supernatural design Creation, or mere chance Evolution? Have you taken the time to ponder and realize how important this is?

_____
_____
_____
_____
_____
_____
_____
_____
_____
_____
_____

6

SUNRISE

*Have you not known? Have you not heard?
The everlasting God, the Lord,
the Creator of the ends of the earth does
not become weary or tired.
His understanding is inscrutable.*
—Isaiah 40:28 NASB

*O*ne early morning while driving on an eastbound highway on my way to work, I had to reach for my sunglasses and pull down the visor. I was suddenly blinded by the fiery glow of the rising sun on the horizon directly in front of me. This wasn't the first time I had experienced a bright sunrise right in front of me while driving; what was different was the realization of the simplicity and importance of this event.

I marveled at the absolute consistency of it all. *Here we go,* I thought. *The sun's coming up again—and right on time—just as it did yesterday, every day last week, every day last month, and every day last year. Actually, the sun has come up on the east horizon at about the same time ever since the sun lit up the sky at the very beginning. Is that awesome or what?*

Of course, we all know that the rotation of the earth is what makes it seem like the sun comes up in the east. If you stood in space just above the North Pole, looking down at the earth, you would observe that it rotates in a counterclockwise direction about its north–south axis. Each revolution of the earth takes twenty-four hours to complete. As we stand or drive on the earth's surface, we're actually rotating *with* the earth. This explains why every twenty-four hours, every morning, we get to see the sun come up at about the same time. As we continue to rotate with the earth, the sun just appears to be moving across the sky from sunrise in the east to sunset in the west.

I bring up the simplicity of a typical sunrise because we sometimes take it for granted, but this daily event is nothing short of a miracle. The show is free for everyone to enjoy, and it's asolutely magnificent. Every morning, the sun has come up for centuries. Every day is another opportunity for humans all over the earth to wake up, look toward the east, see the daylight brought on by the rising sun, and be reassured that something—or Someone—is in complete control of this massive undertaking. This doesn't just happen by accident.

The sun is still shining in the sky today, we think. *The earth must have maintained its rotational speed while we were asleep during the night. The moon is still up there too. The movement of the tides are still churning the waters of the seas across the globe. The clouds continue to float above the earth, painting a continuously changing view on the sky's canvas as if in slow motion. Everything is okay.*

I have to believe that there comes a time in all our lives when we tend to wonder how that happens and how it all started, and perhaps even question why. Whether people wake up in a big city or in a small village located in a different part of the globe, a sunrise is just as magnificent for everyone who takes a moment to ponder and marvel at the sight. Every sunrise is a daily miracle, and we're all privileged beyond description to be able to witness it. Needless to say, it would be foolish for anyone to take this marvelous event for granted as if it's just another daily coincidence.

So what do you think? If you're considering the evolution theory, did the evolution of the rising sun—the rotation of the earth—stop evolving after it reached the twenty-four-hour interval? Is it reasonable to think that there was a time when the sun came up every twenty-three hours? How about every twenty-five hours? What explanation can there be for the precision and consistency of the sun's rise every twenty-four hours over the past thousands of years? Let me suggest that it takes less faith to believe that every magnificent sunrise is the direct result of just one small piece of a very specific grand design by none other than the supernatural Creator of the universe Himself. He made it just so since the beginning.

Where you stand on this topic matters greatly. Do you think it is more likely that the sun comes up right on time every morning due to mere coincidence without anything or anyone in control of it, or do you think it is more likely that it continues to shine consistently as the direct result of a supernatural being—God—keeping it in place while the earth rotates? Every sunrise is a reminder that the big picture is intact. Every sunrise signifies the start of a new day, and as such, a new opportunity to seek the One who keeps it all together in ways we can neither fathom nor possibly understand.

During the most recent centuries, people all over the globe have designed, engineered, and built homes with furniture, dishwashers, refrigerators, and stoves for everyone's improved comfort. We've designed and built cars, computers, telescopes, microscopes, ships, trains, planes, and rockets that allow us to explore other places.

Like never before, we have a greater understanding of everything around us, including the tiniest living DNA molecule mechanisms for individual living species. We've had the privilege of discovering how truly unique our planet Earth really is. We've done all this by utilizing nature's constant laws, which were there from the beginning, as well as scientific formulas discovered through experimentation. We count on these constants to remain this way, and we wonder how they came to be this precise.

All the natural resources we used for these developments were found right here on our planet. We also combined some of these resources to develop other materials to suit our needs. Among the many constant laws of nature, the importance of the gravitational pull of the earth being and remaining constant cannot and should not be underestimated. Who can possibly begin to explain how that natural force came to be?

People build *stuff*. We create things using what is available to us, while taking advantage of existing constant forces found in nature. We turn ideas into designs, then obtain the materials needed to build prototypes that result in useable products. We're creative and constantly striving to improve the products we build.

What if we didn't do any of that? What if we simply allowed all the natural resources to remain where they happen to be? Can anyone imagine the possibility of any of these materials somehow coming together or evolving, on their own, into something useful like a car or a house, given enough time? A person who would seriously make such a claim would be described as unreasonable, among other choice adjectives. Does a car or a house have a chance of understanding its designer? Obviously, people deliberately and specifically designed and created these things.

Now let's go back and consider the daily sunrise example again. None of us can possibly understand how the sun came into existence, or the earth or any living being. What we can all agree on is that we're all witnesses of our existence; we can see, we can hear, we can research, we can think for ourselves, and we can reason.

We cannot scientifically "prove" how the sun was designed and came into existence, nor can we scientifically "prove" what or who is maintaining it. What I personally know for sure is that

I'm in awe when I see a sunrise. It's an obvious reminder for me that I am fortunate enough to witness the workings of this grand, majestic design, live and in full color, right in front of my eyes.

When a sunrise is observed by any of us on any given morning, it is reasonable to say that what we're witnessing is in perfect harmony with the earth and all the other planets in our solar system. Every sunrise can only have been this precise and consistent if it was purposefully intended, planned, designed, created, and placed just so by a supernatural being who is beyond our understanding.

Reflection Questions

Who do you choose to listen to and believe when it comes to an explanation for the origin of the sun which comes up daily?

_____
_____
_____
_____
_____
_____
_____
_____
_____
_____
_____
_____
_____
_____
_____
_____
_____

7

SCIENCE FICTION OR SUPERNATURAL REALITY

God stretches the northern sky over empty space and hangs the earth on nothing.
—*Job 26:7 NLT*

*D*id you ever try to get a straight answer from someone regarding planet Earth's suspension in midair, situated where it happens to be within the vast space all around us? I mean, what holds it up there while it's rotating on its axis once every twenty-four hours and traveling around the sun in precise orbit once every twelve months? Sure, we've all heard about the gravity-attraction-among-masses explanation as well as the balance between centripetal and centrifugal motion, but where did these forces come from originally and what keeps them in place? Can anyone explain this amazing phenomenon to your satisfaction? Does anyone's explanation scientifically prove how everything lined up just so, for things to be the way they are?

We are rotating at a speed of about 1,000 miles per hour, standing at the equator of the earth. I mentioned earlier that the earth is constantly rotating on its north–south axis. The distance around the equator, which is the circumference of the earth, is roughly 24,000 miles. Since it takes twenty-four hours for the earth to make one complete revolution, someone on the equator will have traveled the entire distance of the circumference—24,000 miles—within that twenty-four-hour period at a speed of 1,000 miles per hour.

The earth, while rotating on its north–south axis on a daily basis, is also on a journey circling the sun, moving through space at a speed of about 18.5 miles per second or roughly 67,000 miles per hour. (By comparison, a bullet travels at only about 1,700 miles per hour.) The time it takes the earth to completely travel one time around the sun is twelve months. Within this one-year period, the distance covered by the earth during this one trip is close to 600 million miles. In other words, while standing on the earth's equator, we are actually spinning, due to the earth's daily rotation, at 1,000 miles per hour, while simultaneously rocketing through space at about 67,000 miles per hour due to the earth's yearly orbit around the sun.

We're all travelers, but we may not all realize the extent of the miles we clock every year. No frequent-flyer miles are issued by anyone for this involuntary travel. Just for fun, if you want to calculate how far you've traveled in your life to date, just multiply your age by an approximate 608,760,000 miles per year as shown below:

- Distance traveled due to earth's rotation = 1,000 miles/hour x 24 hours/day x 365 days/year = 8,760,000 miles/year.
- Distance traveled due to earth's orbit around the sun = 600,000,000 miles/year.

- Therefore, the total distance traveled per year = 8,760,000 + 600,000,000 = 608,760,000 miles/year.
- I'm 57 years old. To date, I've traveled about 34.7 billion miles, calculated as 57 years x 608,760,000 miles/year = 34.7 billion miles.

The good news is that we don't notice this rapid motion. The earth's gravity force ensures that the inhabitants as well as the atmosphere surrounding the earth all remain firmly in place while moving through space.

To take this a step further, our solar system—within which planet Earth resides—is only one out of tens of billions of other solar systems, all of which make up our Milky Way. The Milky Way, complete with its billions of solar systems, rotates like a pinwheel in space at a speed of about 500,000 miles per hour. It is so massive that even at that high rotation speed, our solar system would take about 230 million years to complete just one revolution around the Milky Way.

While we're here, I might as well note that the Milky Way also has an overall motion through the vast space of the universe at speeds reported to 3.3 million miles per hour. According to the best estimates of astronomers, there are at least 100 billion galaxies in the observable universe.

To summarize, if you were standing at the equator of the earth, you would actually be moving:

- 1,000 miles/hour due to the daily rotation of the earth about its north–south axis.
- 67,000 miles/hour due to the yearly orbit of the earth around the sun.
- 500,000 miles/hour due to the spinning of the Milky Way containing our solar system along with the tens of billions of other solar systems.

- 3,300,000 miles/hour due to overall motion of the Milky Way through space.

These are mind-staggering numbers, and that's just the start. When thinking about what we've learned about our universe to date, our imaginations are stretched as far as we can fathom. In order to even attempt to describe the vast distances across our universe and in between galaxies in space, we need to use the speed of light traveling for some amount of time.

We've come to understand that light travels at a speed of approximately 186,000 miles per second. To give you a sense of how fast that is, you'd reach the sun in about 8 minutes and 20 seconds traveling at the speed of light. Now try to imagine being strapped to the tip of a light beam as it is turned on. Also try to imagine being able to hang on for the durations shown below—traveling at the speed of light—to see the distance you've traveled:

- One second later = 186,000 miles = equivalent distance of about 7.5 times around the earth.
- One hour later = 186,000 miles/second x 60 seconds/minute x 60 minutes/hour = 669,600,000 miles.
- One day later = 669,600,000 miles/hour x 24 hours/day = 16,070,400,000 miles.
- One week later = 16,070,400,000 miles/day x 7 days/week = 112,492,800,000 miles.
- One year later = 112,492,800,000 miles/week x 52 weeks/year = 5,849,625,600,000 miles.

Said another way (and rounding it off), if you were to travel at the speed of light for a period of one year, one light year = about 6 trillion miles in distance. Our Milky Way measures about 100,000 light years in diameter = 600,000 trillion miles.

Can you imagine traveling at the speed of light for 100,000 years continuously? If you can, you will have only traveled from one end our Milky Way to the other. The known universe is estimated to span about 30 billion light years. Needless to say, it's unimaginably vast. It's beyond measure.

Mankind has developed the technology to be able to see incredibly far out in space. The history of the Hubble Space Telescope is truly fascinating. Unfortunately, we've only just begun to scratch the surface of outer space discovery. We keep looking in order to gain further understanding of how the planets of outer space formed, with the hope that we'll be able to logically explain how life began here on earth. We seem to be in constant search for the next big discovery, looking for that certain something out there that just might resemble conditions similar to those on our planet. We're tirelessly searching for that magical formula we know has to exist in order to sustain life.

The fact remains that the more telescopes and manned and unmanned rocket-propelled missions we send out into space, the more we discover how truly unique we are here on earth. The more we learn of the details and immeasurable vastness of the universe, the more we gain understanding and should be absolutely amazed by how small yet utterly remarkable our planet is.

Given the countless galaxies, stars, and solar systems we already know of, try to approach a math teacher, a scientist, or an astronaut about the coincidences that had to have taken place for our planet to evolve by mere chance in such a way so as to sustain life for countless individual living species. Challenge yourself to engage in a meaningful common-sense discussion about the probability of such coincidences taking place without any outside intelligence or influence whatsoever. Then compare the infinitesimally small probability with that of winning the lottery, which would likely seem gargantuan. Try to honestly fathom the possibility of such coincidences coming together on their own somehow. How much faith would it take to believe in such meaningless randomness?

All of human ingenuity throughout history, combined with persistence to find answers from our universe, continues to provide evidence that demonstrates with increased clarity that there is order in the universe. Natural laws have been discovered. The reality of the existence of our solar system, complete with life on earth as we can all observe, is undoubtedly unexplainable to our mortal satisfaction. We cannot explain logically how this all came into being. It is obviously not science fiction since we're here and we're all real.

However, there is a viable alternative option that is opposite the concept of imaginary science-fiction evolutionary theory of existence: There had to have been a supernatural, specific, purposeful, designer behind all of what we know exists.

It's supernatural creation, which in my humble opinion requires far less faith to believe as the method responsible for the beginning of everything.

Within the entire universe, as vast as it is, we continue to discover that our planet Earth is the only one that's as remarkable as we've discovered it to be. We can also reasonably conclude that the one and only Creator—God—also designed human beings with intelligence, reason, and common sense. It's as if He wanted us to look far out into space, He wanted us to learn about every discovery in our vast universe, and He wanted us to know in our hearts that He is far beyond our understanding.

He certainly succeeded.

Reflection Questions

Have you looked in the mirror lately and tried to imagine the possibility of this amazing life-sustaining planet Earth somehow assembling itself by mere randomness?

_____
_____
_____
_____
_____
_____
_____
_____

Why is your answer logical?

_____
_____
_____
_____
_____
_____

Does it not make more sense that a supernatural being (which we cannot possibly understand) was responsible for this awesome design?

_____
_____
_____
_____
_____
_____
_____

8

SEEKING TRUTH—THE ORIGIN OF EVERYTHING

The fool says in his heart, "There is no God."
—*Psalm 14:1 ESV*

So which is it? Does God really exist or not? What is the truth? I've heard it said that you can't persuade someone about the truth if they're determined to believe a lie.

Human beings in general seem to wrestle with the reality of what we see, hear, and observe from the day we were born. This process tends to be a unique experience as we each analyze the information we constantly soak up. From early in life, we're curious about the nature of things, so we explore to gain understanding. Some things are taught to us by family, teachers, or mentors, while other things are learned through trial and error. Our education of life continues as we mature and gather information. As time passes, we're bombarded with a multitude of possibilities, claims, and theories offering explanations of events as being true.

The need for belief in something to be true seems to stem from within the core and essence of our human nature. It's how we are all wired. This truth we seek also seems to be necessary for us to function in a normal way. The outcome of every passing day, week, month, and year tends to be shaped and influenced by what we believe to be true, whether we realize it or not.

Countless books and articles have been written on the meaning of life, by scholars and philosophers, as well as self-proclaimed experts on the subject. My intention is not to add to such a list. Instead, it's to simply chime in with the hope that we all make better use of the amazing attribute we're all born with—common sense—when pondering the big picture and meaning of our existence.

The thoughts we generate within our minds, the words we speak, and the actions we take every day are directly connected to the things we believe as true. To put it bluntly, truth is immensely important to our sanity. Ultimately, I want to reveal the all-important consequences resulting from the individualized free-will choices we all make, based on these principles, every day.

When we allow ourselves to look in the mirror with honest self-reflection, we get closer to realizing that our number of days on earth are relatively brief. As such, we all strive to improve our own lives as well as the lives of others around us, to the best of our abilities, by somehow making every day count in a positive way. At some point, we may even conclude that our brief existence on this unique planet was no accident at all, even if we don't fully understand our purpose at the time.

Within the private places of our minds, we prefer to think of ourselves as generally good, and it's important for us to be known and remembered by others as such. At the same time, we also feel the need to feel loved, accepted, valuable, useful, respected, and appreciated for our efforts. To say we're complicated would be a huge understatement.

From early in human history, the Bible and its teachings have served as the source of truth with respect to the origin of everything. The Bible teaches that there was always a perfect and holy God in eternity past and He will continue to exist in eternity future. The Bible also teaches that when time—as we know it to exist—first began, God created the heavens, the earth, all life forms, and everything that exists: "In the beginning God created the heavens and the earth" (Genesis 1:1).

Besides being eternal and all-powerful, God's other biblical attributes include being all-knowing, sovereign, omnipresent, immutable, dependable, consistent, righteous, merciful, just, holy, and true.

God accomplished all of creation by speaking it into existence, and the Bible claims that the one and only true God designed and created it all. He is the originator of all galaxies, all solar systems, and all planets, including this extraordinary planet we live on, Earth. He designed and created the land and waters as well as the atmosphere with all the necessary components to sustain life. He designed and created all living creatures to be able to procreate according to their species. Ultimately, He designed and created the very first human beings—Adam and Eve—in His own image with a free will and an eternal living spirit.

Of course, this is where our minds go into tilt mode. God certainly knew that we, as mere mortals, could not begin to understand this speaking-everything-into-existence stuff, so the Bible teaches that we must believe it by faith. This belief by faith plays a key role because we're expected to trust what the Bible teaches as being true. In essence, the Bible claims that God Himself is the author and He has left His us His Word—the Bible—as a sort of autobiography.

History shows that despite numerous attempts by mankind to destroy the Bible—and by default, all of its teachings—this incredible book survived all internal and external challenges every time. God's Word is still here and available for us to get to know

Him personally. He wants for us to know the truth about the origin of everything, how we got to where we are currently, and the final destination of everything.

So what's all the fuss about anyway? Why would mankind—generation after generation—want to suppress and even destroy the Bible, especially if it's true? Much has been written about this, but the simple answer is that man loves sin and doesn't want to be held accountable to a perfectly just and holy God.

The first two people on earth, Adam and Eve, chose not to trust God's Word. They instead chose to believe the lies of Satan, so they fell into a depraved state from being deceived. As a result, all generations that followed were infected with this sinful condition. The flawed, prideful nature of mankind caused people to quickly sink deep into the darkness of unspeakable sin, thereby rejecting the Bible and its teachings.

Over time, the sinful nature of mankind continued to lure people further and further away from biblical teachings. We wanted to make the rules and live in any way that pleased us without guilt of conscience. People became increasingly more hostile to God, thereby bringing everything into question, including the biblical account of creation itself.

Charles Darwin's *On the Origin of Species* was originally published in November of 1859. Essentially, Darwin introduced the theory that all living species came into existence over the course of long periods of time through the process of natural selection and a sort of survival of the fittest. In other words, he was determined to explain how we all got here and thus gain notoriety within the scientific community, while discounting the need for God. Obviously, challenges and counter-arguments were made to Darwin's claims, so he continued to revise his documented theory. It's no surprise that the controversies created by his theories have yet to cease.

Darwin was born in 1809, and to this day he is credited as being the person who introduced the idea that life, as we know it to exist, evolved over time. He began working on his theory of evolution in the early 1830s before publishing his first edition in 1859. The second edition was then published in 1860, the third in 1861, the fourth in 1866, the fifth 1869, and the sixth and final edition in 1872. For this last edition, perhaps in an effort to make it sound more definitive, or perhaps in a desperate attempt to convince the masses, Darwin omitted the title's first word, *On*. Perhaps he believed the new title, *The Origin of Species,* would make a difference for his struggling hypothesis.

Although Darwin avoided specific explanation of human origins, he maintained his theory that there had to have been a struggle for existence of living organisms, thus the concept of survival of the fittest. However, this speculation fails to account for the origin of life in the first place. It was nothing more than imagination suggesting gradual changes of basic nonliving chemical elements developing into complex replicating living molecules. Darwin expected everyone to simply believe what cannot be accomplished by trained scientists with the most sophisticated equipment in the most controlled laboratory environments on earth today. Oh, and this all had to have begun somehow by blind chance a billion years ago.

Despite his observations and work over the course of about forty years, there was very limited molecular understanding in the science community at that time. As a result, one of many hurdles he had to overcome was the inference that over the course of a long time, mutations and natural selections in living organisms must have occurred in such a way as to turn an amoeba into the earth's living species as we know them today.

In other words, Darwin presented a theory proposing that humans (as well as all other complex living species) all originated as basic, tiny organisms that miraculously appeared somehow, somewhere, at some point in the distant past. He expected people to believe that every aspect of all necessary living cells of organs within a living body not only evolved into existence but also somehow organized themselves over the course of many eons, in such a way so as to form a functioning living creature. Evolution theory is a matter of faith, not science.

Many scientific discoveries have been established since 1859. Despite mankind's relentless efforts to prove evolution, and thus to resist the authority of a supernatural Creator, each new scientific discovery points directly toward purposeful, unique, intelligent design. If Darwin were alive today and had the advantage of understanding the unique nature of living organisms structured around the remarkable DNA molecule (which was not available in 1859), do you honestly believe that he would still make such an evolutionary claim about the origin of species? All scientific facts support special creation, not evolution.

This is about as simplistic as it gets. It is the beginning of the journey to becoming a citizen of heaven. What's your choice? What do you believe with respect to the origin of everything? Do you believe everything you see around you evolved from essentially nothing by mere chance, or do you believe that everything around you was created by a supernatural God? No doubt, both scenarios require faith. Only one scenario can possibly be true.

Just imagine the complexities of the human body—a beating heart, blood vessels, electrical brain impulses, eyesight, sense of smell, the nervous system, the skeletal frame, muscle tissue, hormones, emotions, the ability to reason, and the reproductive and digestive systems, just to name a few. Either they all somehow came together by chance over eons of elapsed time, or these same complex body organs were all purposefully designed and supernaturally created to function as intended by the God of the Bible at a specific point in time in the garden of Eden.

Your perspective on life itself, and your level of understanding about every event that happens in the world around you, is directly influenced by this critical decision, whether you realize it or not. If you choose to believe by faith that God's creation is the true origin of everything, then congratulations. You've taken the first step toward obtaining citizenship in heaven.

REFLECTION QUESTIONS

Do you really want to know the truth about creation and evolution?

Are you willing to pursue it until you are sure?

Will you give God a chance to reveal Himself to you? Do you realize that God is truth?

9

VALUE, PURPOSE, AND THE FUTURE

For what will it profit a man if he gains the whole world, and loses his own soul?
—Mark 8:36

What is humanity truly worth, and why do we all want to accumulate stuff while here on earth? What does the future look like after we've lived our last days on earth?

Other than doing our very best to improve our personal standard of living, there seems to be no universally accepted level where enough is enough. This is neither published, nor taught, nor fully understood, nor agreed upon by society at large. The spectrum of living standards couldn't be wider, as some people live their lives in poverty while others abuse excess in wasteful ways.

Who is the authority of a person's true value anyway? Who gets to decide how life is to be measured—according to what scale or standard? We can probably safely agree that a person's life on earth, irrespective of their current status, will be enriched when helping someone else in need. Something takes place within all of us that is rewarding when we know we've helped another person in some way.

Furthermore, from a similar point of view, a time comes when we look all around us and wonder if there's a purpose behind all that is happening. Although helping someone else can be very satisfying, you might also find yourself wondering about your specific purpose in life. After all, you're going about your own business, living out your days with family, friends, and coworkers, and perhaps even taking time to also help others along the way.

But what happens when that's over? Was it all somehow worth the effort? Did we fulfill our purpose? Time continues to march forward. Whether we like it or not, whether we are prepared or not, we will all face the reality that our physical existence on earth is temporary, while our souls are permanent and live forever. Right after we take our last breath here on earth, each of our eternal souls will face the consequences of our beliefs while alive in our physical bodies.

At some point in time, either in the quiet moments of our private thoughts or in more public places, we have all engaged into a debate about when, why, and even how it all began. How big is this universe that it contains countless galaxies? How big is each of these galaxies that they contain innumerable stars and celestial bodies? Why is our tiny planet so uniquely situated within our solar system that it can sustain life? Why is it so different? How, when, and why did life on earth begin? The answers to these questions will vary by person, but we can all agree that life itself is certainly very special and can be considered a miracle.

Looking at the human race, you might be able to reason that people of all nations should be able to agree on what the future has in store for us. After all, we're all here right now and our ancestors got here somehow. It also goes without saying that the occupation of our planet by birds, fish, animals, and human beings had to have started at some point in time.

The same rationale of origins can be applied by looking out into space as far as we can see. The earth itself, along with the moon, the sun, the other eight planets within our solar system, the billions of stars and planets within our Milky Way, and the other billions of galaxies within this immeasurable universe, all had to have come into existence by some means with a specific beginning.

There can be only one explanation for the origin of everything that we can possibly see and know to exist. Given that, we also know that intelligent people from centuries ago, as well as from current generations, have written numerous books and articles offering explanations and theories on the subject of origins, thereby giving people options to choose from.

When visiting a new city, you might get asked by the locals where are you from. It's normal conversation. You know where you were born, and you know how you arrived where you live now, and you know the places you visited throughout your life. On a much bigger scale, it also makes sense to ask where all of humanity came from and how we got to where we are. Of greatest importance, however, is our destination. Where are we all headed in the future?

Knowing where one is headed will depend on each person's understanding of where we've all come from. Irrespective of the number of explanations being offered, irrespective of the popularity of the person having verbalized or written about a particular position, and irrespective of how many people accept or reject any of the explanations of the origin of all things, the fact remains that only one explanation can possibly be true. In other words, we should all be able to agree that all that exists came into being by a specific and unique process. We should also be able to agree that only one of all the explanations being offered for these origins can be the correct option.

People everywhere are busy providing the daily needs for their families and planning a more secure future, all while striving toward more fulfilling relationships with others in their circle of influence. While doing their best to maintain this balancing act of daily activities, most people will admit that we all possess a curiosity deep inside, wondering what the truth is about where we're headed after life on earth ends. What will that future look like, and where will we all fit in? But despite the common features and interconnections among humanity, complete agreement on our future destination is nowhere to be found.

Most people say they want to know what the future holds. Some even invest time and money into interpretations of star formations or cards, advice from fortune tellers, or the performing of ancient rituals. Others simply rely on beliefs from their ancestors passed down through generations. These same individuals also tend to quickly sway in different directions according to fads, popular polls, TV shows, and influential people's personal views, not really investigating the validity of the information they accept as being true.

It would stand to reason, then, that the differences in peoples' opinions and beliefs about future destinations after death are a direct result of not being able to agree on a common starting point for humanity. Considering the extraordinary divide among people of all nations as to the origin of mankind, it is not surprising at all that people's points of view about the future can be totally different as well.

Even so, this wasn't how it was meant to be. Unfortunately, we all tend to follow the crowd to some degree. There's less resistance when going with the flow. Many people dismiss thinking about the future at all. Sure, we've all heard about heaven and hell, but who really knows, right? *After all, I'm a good person,* they reason, and quickly conclude, *I think I'll end up on the right side.* Sadly, others think there's just nothingness after death. They figure this life on earth is all there is, so they might as well live it up.

The fact remains that most people continue to be deceived by the few who wanted selfish notoriety, such as Darwin. This deceptive theory about the beginning, has unfortunately been generally accepted in spite of recent DNA discoveries. Acceptance by the masses has in turn completely distorted most people's understanding on what happens after death, discounting the gravity of their decision.

To most, the present is all that matters. They spend their time pursuing gold, silver, and all kinds of worldly possessions, and don't even bother to investigate the importance of the origin of the beginning for themselves, thus clouding their understanding of the future after death. Sadly, many choose to remain in a state of ignorance.

I hope what you've read so far encourages you to humble yourself and seek divine wisdom on this most-important subject. You can absolutely have the confidence knowing, by faith, that in the beginning, mankind and all living creatures were designed by a supernatural Creator—the God of the Bible—for a specific purpose here on earth. You can also rest peacefully every night, knowing in your heart that the eternal future of your soul will be secure in heaven once life on earth ends. Take the time to seek God for yourself, and discover the joy of being reassured of your future destination.

Reflection Questions

Do you believe you have immeasurable value no matter what your current status happens to be. Do you realize that God has a purpose for your life?

_____
_____
_____
_____
_____
_____
_____
_____
_____

What would you like your future to look like?

_____
_____
_____
_____
_____
_____
_____
_____
_____
_____

10
FAITH AND FOUNDATIONS

But seek first the kingdom of God and His righteousness, and all these things will be added unto you.
—Matthew 6:33 ESV

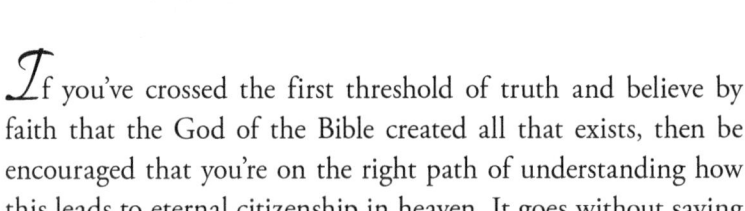

*I*f you've crossed the first threshold of truth and believe by faith that the God of the Bible created all that exists, then be encouraged that you're on the right path of understanding how this leads to eternal citizenship in heaven. It goes without saying that merely standing still on this path—professing that God created everything—will not get you there. Keep moving forward and learning more about the holy nature of God, and you'll know for sure what it takes to be in His presence.

Matthew 5:8 says, "Blessed are the pure in heart, for they shall see God" (ESV). I've heard it said that the heart of the matter is a matter of the heart. So if you believe that the God of the Bible created everything that exists, and if you seek Him to discover His character, you will desire to purify your heart in order to see Him in heaven.

We all tend to display a particular image while out in public or even with family members. We want everyone to think we've got our act together—as much as possible—even though we all know that everyone struggles with personal challenges. More importantly, the things we think, say, and do when no one is watching, reveal the realistic condition of our heart. Do we cheat in any way, steal the smallest of items, embellish the truth, tell "white" lies, or perhaps visit places we couldn't go with our spouse? Needless to say, there's room for improvement when it comes to what's really going on within the depths of our hearts.

The expression *one step at a time* now comes to mind. We all need to put one foot in front of the other to get from point A to point B, so now what? Where do we go from here? How do we get from the present condition of our hearts to one that is pure in the sight of God? We get easily distracted because *life happens,* as the saying goes. We work to support our families, and we need food, clothing, and shelter to survive on this planet. We also get involved in all kinds of other activities and interests that vie for our attention and occupy our time.

A natural progression of events is revealed to us in the pages of the Bible to help us gain understanding of God. He has revealed how everything began (in Genesis) and He has revealed how everything will end (in Revelation), along with everything else in between, including His merciful plan to grant us access in heaven for eternity. God does not want us to merely acknowledge His existence and that He is the author of creation. He wants us to also get to know Him personally so that our hearts will be transformed.

Learning about something or someone always requires will. We've all been designed with free will, so learning something new must be willingly pursued. A teacher is completely ineffective if the student isn't willing to learn, regardless of the value of teacher's lesson.

The next step is to learn more about God. He just wants us to get to know who He is, so we can have the assurance that He's fully aware of our needs and the desires of our hearts. After all, He designed each of us as a unique masterpiece and He knows everything about us. He advises us to seek Him first so that everything else in our lives falls into place, as intended for our own good.

If you were to order a custom-built house to be your family's permanent residence on earth, you'd want to know about the designer himself. As well, a house designer with an impeccable reputation would want to provide his resume to you to put your mind at ease. It's in your best interest to know that the designer is not only of excellent character but also has the credentials needed to design a stable house for you.

No matter how good the house may look on the outside when it's new, and no matter how persistent and polished the salesperson may be when the house is sold to you, it's in your best interest to get to know the designer as well as the builder. Suffice it to say that a house built according to the specifications of an unqualified, shady designer would soon crack, shift, and may even crumble. If the foundation was designed with sheer ignorance or with the influence of uneducated opinions, then a disastrous outcome would be a sure bet.

A new house can appear quite sturdy from a distance. But the most critical factor when considering the stability and longevity of this house is the foundation. The materials used, the dimensions of the footings, the type of soil and weather conditions of the area, and the workmanship of the construction must be taken into account by the designer. The stability and longevity of the house depend on it.

Similarly, God—the supernatural designer and builder of everything—wants us to learn about Him as well. It's fundamental, and it makes perfect sense. He wants us to get to know His character, and He wants us to be confident in His amazing skill set. He designed the foundations of the universe and everything in it. Just imagine what it might take to create the earth, which most people simply take for granted. Do you think it's worth your time to be willing to learn more about the earth's original designer?

God wants you to be assured that He will never let you down and that your heart will be transformed if you seek Him earnestly. You'll know this because you'll no longer want to think, say, or do the things of your old nature. He wants to have a relationship with you, for your own good, here on earth as well as in eternal heaven.

From my own personal experience, the more I've sought to understand the character of the Creator of the universe, the more my eyes have opened to see how little I really knew about the magnitude of His grandeur. I've come to realize and appreciate that He has been in the background of my life all along. He has been shining His light in front of me when I was lost, He has carried me when I was too weak to stand, He has provided comfort for me when I was alone and without hope, and He has protected and picked me up when I didn't deserve it.

The God of the Bible is far greater and far more merciful than can be described in words. He is without question worthy of the time and effort we invest to seek Him and learn of His flawless, holy character.

Reflection Questions

Do you realize that God is infinite?

Are you prioritizing above all things to discover who God is so that you can be sure that He is in control of absolutely everything?

11

GOD'S AMAZING LOVE

"For God so loved the word, that He gave His only Son, that whoever believes in Him should not perish but have eternal life."
—John 3:16 ESV

Love, as a noun, can be described as an intense feeling of deep affection. I've heard it said that the greatest experience we can have is to love and be loved in return. Love overlooks flaws, imperfections, and even downright hostility. It causes us to protect the ones we love. If you've ever had the privilege of loving someone, you've likely sacrificed in order to show your love for that person.

If you're a parent, you have a natural sense of love toward your kids. Most parents will do just about anything to protect their kids from harm. In the animal kingdom, you'll see similar behaviors of affection, protection, and sacrifice. All this, of course, is our innate behavior to preserve our well-being here on earth.

But what about afterward? What happens to our eternal souls after our physical bodies are no longer breathing? Who is able to do anything about the kind of love and sacrifice needed to protect and preserve our eternal souls?

If you profess to believe in God's eternal existence and His supernatural creation of all things, then you have concluded that the Bible is God's Word and biblical teaching is as true as He is. Furthermore, if you've earnestly learned about God's character and holy nature, then you've discovered that there are only two possible destinations—heaven or hell—where a person's eternal soul can end up.

Adam and Eve disobeyed God in the garden of Eden when they ate of the forbidden fruit. As a result, all of mankind became tainted in the sight of God. History shows that people became progressively more and more depraved, committing ugly, unspeakable acts toward one another as well as toward God Himself. Because of this perpetual fallen state, the innermost fibers of a person's heart need transformation for the eternal soul to end up in God's holy presence in heaven forever. The Bible teaches that if this transformation of the heart doesn't happen, the soul will end up in the eternal lake of fire.

So how can the transformation of a person's heart take place so the eternal soul can go to heaven? This is where God's amazing love comes in. The Bible teaches that for humanity's fallen nature to be rescued from eternal suffering in the lake of fire, God's own Son Jesus paid the price and suffered in our place to save all who believe. The magnitude of this sacrifice has been, and continues to be, God's amazing grace and love toward people, who naturally want to reject Him.

At Christmastime, we celebrate the birth of God's Son Jesus, who was born to Virgin Mary some two thousand years ago. We exchange gifts, but the true meaning of Christmas is God's greatest gift to humanity through the birth of His Son. God's extraordinary plan for our eternal salvation was to sacrifice His only Son, even though none of us deserve such mercy. No greater gift, no greater kind of love, can possibly exist.

Jesus lived a perfect life without sin. He showed Himself to be both human and deity, having performed miracles among men. He was despised by most and then betrayed all according to God's prophesy. Jesus suffered beyond human comprehension and was ultimately crucified. Easter depicts His death and resurrection on the third day, indicating that death itself had been conquered and eternal life is available to all who believe.

John 14:6 says, "Jesus answered, 'I am the way and the truth and the life. No one comes to the Father except through me'" (NIV). The Bible teaches that our only path to reach eternal heaven was made possible by God's grace alone, through faith in Jesus alone. It goes on to tells us that we must humble ourselves, repent of our fallen ways, and ask for God's grace to intervene. The only way for our depraved hearts to be transformed is for us to recognize, by faith, that the life, death, and resurrection of Jesus have provided the only path to heaven.

The challenge now is to look in the mirror and ask yourself, "Is Jesus precious me? Do I really know Him? Do I really appreciate the magnitude of His sacrifice and the immeasurable value of the gift He provided for me?" If you're honest, you'll find the answers within your heart.

It really doesn't matter if you go to church, if you teach Sunday school, if you're a good person, or if you run a charitable foundation. What matters for citizenship in heaven is a personal relationship with Jesus, God's Son. It's never too late to get to know Him better, while you still can, for your own good.

Reflection Questions

Do you realize that God's son Jesus made it possible for anyone to end up in heaven?

_____
_____
_____
_____
_____
_____
_____
_____

Have you pondered on the magnitude of the sacrifice Jesus paid in full for your sinful nature, in order for you to be in God's presence in heaven for eternity?

_____
_____
_____
_____
_____
_____
_____
_____

Have you thanked Him for it? Have you asked for God's guidance going forward?

_____
_____
_____
_____
_____
_____
_____
_____

12

EVERYDAY MIRACLES IN PLAIN SIGHT

The heavens declare the glory of God, and the sky above proclaims his handiwork.
—*Psalm 19:1 ESV*

The world we live in is full of miracles, and they're all on display—every moment of every day—for us to marvel at. Some examples include:

- At sea level, water freezes at 32 degrees Fahrenheit (0 degrees Celsius) and boils at 212 degrees Fahrenheit (100 degrees Celsius).
- Oxygen levels decrease at higher elevations.
- The force of gravity on the earth is precise, and we know it exists because we are always pulled back toward its surface at the same rate.
- The moon is held by a constant force while revolving around the earth—without flying away into space—and

it causes massive amounts of water to wash up and down shorelines to churn the oceans, forming clouds that produce rain.
- The earth spins on its axis once every twenty-four hours, consistently resulting in daytime and nighttime.
- The earth's rotational axis is tilted at 23.5 degrees and is maintained as it revolves around the sun, without leaving its orbit, once every twelve months, creating the four seasons we experience, and preventing temperature extremes anywhere on the planet.
- Carrots always have been and always will be orange.
- Apple trees grow over time and produce other apples.
- Dolphins can produce only baby dolphins.
- Turtles can produce only baby turtles.
- Eagles can produce only baby eagles.
- Humming birds can produce only baby humming birds.
- Tigers can produce only baby tigers.
- Giraffes can produce only baby giraffes.
- Polar bears can produce only baby polar bears.
- Human beings can produce only baby human beings.

All of nature declares God's glory and majesty, all by supreme design. The evidence of supernatural creation of all living creatures according to their kind is obvious everywhere we look. Nothing is hidden, and no specialized education is required to see that. Everything is able to be seen, observed, examined, and marveled at.

Stop and give your thoughts a chance to catch up with what's happening every day, right in front of your eyes. We're so privileged to have front-row seats to witness every facet of life unfold just the way God designed it from the very beginning.

We're all walking on a remarkable spherical surface—planet Earth—which is suspended by seemingly nothing, in the vastness of space and among countless other planets. We're kept from freezing by the warmth of the sun, which continues to burn from the day it was lit in the sky. We're all breathing the air that blankets our planet with just the right amount of oxygen for our brains and bodies to function as intended. Our hearts are pre-programmed to pump blood, which replenishes itself if lost, to all the living organs within our bodies to sustain life.

We're all witnessing new births of living creatures, all within their species, on this same amazing planet. There is order and intelligent design in all living things, and it's impossible for these things to have simply appeared from nothing by mere coincidence over time. These are supernatural designed miracles we should *not* take for granted. God alone is the author of all of creation, and He is immeasurably worthy to be studied, pursued, loved, praised, believed, worshiped, and feared.

Reflection Questions

Have you dared to ask God to open your eyes so you can "see" and believe the magnificent miracles of His work, which are on full display every day?

_____
_____
_____
_____
_____
_____
_____
_____
_____

What are you afraid of?

_____
_____
_____
_____
_____
_____
_____
_____
_____

13

PROFOUND COURAGE

Whoever acknowledges me before others,
I will also acknowledge before my Father in heaven.
—Matthew 10:32 NIV

It was a theater-like auditorium with a balcony and a stage at the front. To the best of my recollection, we were up in the balcony seats with a group of young people from our church. I am paraphrasing, but after the message, the speaker had a few questions for the audience:

- "Are you willing to soften your heart and open the door?"
- "Jesus is persistently knocking, and He wants you to be assured of the gift of heaven. It's up to you, so will you open the door to your heart and invite Him into your life?"
- "If so, will you make your way to the front stage to show others that you've made the decision and you're not ashamed of it?"

I looked around and noticed my younger sister, Rodica, had tears welling in her eyes. Then she stood up from her seat, excused herself past the others in our row, and went downstairs to the lower level. I believe she was about fifteen at the time. Looking straight ahead and without hesitation, she calmly walked down the aisle toward the stage, where a small group of people gathered. She was the only one from our group who went downstairs.

After a short prayer by the speaker, this group of people near the stage turned around and were greeted by a standing ovation from the audience. They were all publicly declaring that they recognized their need for a greater power to cleanse their soul so they could go to heaven. They openly acknowledged that they needed Jesus and willingly opened their hearts, inviting Him to dwell inside.

I remember thinking that it took profound courage for her to stand up and walk downstairs that night. I didn't talk with her about specific details of what had happened, but I observed a sort of quiet confidence within her afterward. My sister had been courageous enough to humble herself and ask God for His mercy while relying completely in the work of His Son Jesus. As it turned out, her short journey on earth ended when God saw fit to bring her eternal soul to heaven about three years later. I look forward to seeing her again one day.

I've attended a few funerals throughout the years. We do so to pay our respects and offer support to the grieving family on the passing of their loved one. Some funeral services are packed full of people who knew the deceased and want to honor the person one last time. We take our turn walking toward the grieving family, offering our words of condolence, and then (sometimes) viewing the remains of a resting body without a soul in a casket. Beautiful flower arrangements, videos, pictures, light arrangements, candles, even Christmas trees or memorabilia may be nearby. The idea is to bring back fond memories of the person who is no longer with us. It's very nice, for sure.

Citizen of Heaven

When the funeral service begins, the minister, priest, or designated speaker says a few words, then everyone is seated. The service may start with comforting Bible verses where God's mercy for the deceased is brought up. Maybe there will be some customary smoke being scattered around the casket for some traditional reason. Maybe some funny stories will be shared, and some songs may be included as part of the service. It's a somber reminder of the finality of life on earth, so we cope with it to the best of our ability.

I have to confess that unless I know the person who just passed away, I end up looking at the deceased and thinking, *I wonder where he (or she) ended up.* During most funeral services, I find that there is simply no mention of the personal relationship the deceased may have had with Jesus, who alone could have provided access to heaven after death. This would likely be an important topic, especially at the person's funeral, if this personal relationship with God existed. How sad that it's not the case in many instances.

Amid the condolences and stories shared by people who knew the deceased best, statements may be made that the deceased is now looking down and smiling on everyone in attendance, implying that their soul is in heaven. I'm sure everyone there hopes that's the case, but can anyone really know for sure? How much comfort can you imagine that assurance of heaven would bring?

I also hope that the deceased, while alive, had the courage to humble themselves, repent of their sinful nature, and believe that Jesus paid the ultimate price for their access to heaven. I also hope that the deceased, while alive, was not ashamed to acknowledge their association with the Creator's only Son and His sacrifice for all who believe. I have no doubt that if the person truly believed, it would have been demonstrated in the way they lived their life and everyone would have known it. That person would have had God's fingerprints all over their life. Their friends and family would have known it for sure—which would have resulted in a lot of happy tears in the room, with people knowing for sure that the soul of the deceased ended up in heaven.

My younger sister knew she would end up in heaven the moment she began her journey, convicted of her need for Jesus to transform her heart. She was far from perfect, just like the rest of us, but she repented, was forgiven, and was granted citizenship in heaven instantly. Her short life demonstrated humility and honesty in her relationship with Jesus, and I didn't have to wonder about the final destination of her soul when I attended her funeral. I was comforted beyond measure, knowing she ended up in heaven the moment she took her last breath on earth.

I also know that you can have the same assurance. There is no greater inner peace you can experience. The challenge is to have the courage to humble yourself. Recognize your human, fallen, temporary state and your need for divine intervention. Ask Jesus to soften your heart so He can reside inside. Ask Him to forgive you, and earnestly seek His help to transform you heart. Ask for His guidance daily, and know that He will be in your corner to pick you up when you stumble. Nothing is more important for your peace of mind, a meaningful current life on earth, and eternity in heaven afterward.

Reflection Questions

Are you ashamed or overwhelmed with joy when you hear the name of Jesus?

_____
_____
_____
_____
_____
_____
_____
_____
_____
_____

Are you willing to tell others of His love for you?

_____
_____
_____
_____
_____
_____
_____
_____
_____
_____

14

GODLESSNESS

Give ear and hear my voice, listen and hear my speech.
—Isaiah 28:23 NASB

$\mathcal{I}$ once had a university professor who insisted on having his students write down a statement under the title *Problem*, describing in our own words the problem we were given to solve for the weekly assignments. He wanted each student to paraphrase the problems in our own words, even if it sounded similar to how the problem was stated in the textbook.

At first, many of us didn't find value in this since the scenario to be resolved was already written in the textbook. We just wanted to write any appropriate assumptions being made, then go right to the write-up of the solution. After numerous complaints about the extra time it took us to rewrite what already seemed obvious, the professor gave us the explanation behind his reasoning. I've never forgotten what he said, and I'll paraphrase it here:

"You'll find that most people from all walks of life have a difficult time clearly verbalizing, much less describing in written detail, the exact problem in need of resolution. For that reason, it's important that you initiate the solution to the problem by first concisely re-stating your understanding of what the problem is to begin with. By having an accurate understanding of the problem, only then will you have a chance to arrive at the correct answer."

Since that time, I've witnessed countless situations, both personal and professional, when people were working hard to resolve something that turned out to not be the problem at all. They were practically running in circles trying to impress one another, drowning the facts in bureaucracy, pulling some sort of prideful rank against one another without any form of direction or purpose. They certainly seemed busy while discussing, calling, emailing, setting up meetings, and even establishing committees to reach consensus. All were lame attempts to find solutions to issues that were simply not well defined nor clearly understood.

These people often got nowhere fast because they didn't even agree on the issue that needed to be resolved, much less admit to not having an understanding of the problem itself. Of course, if a fresh set of eyes asked for a definition of the problem, that person was practically ridiculed and often met with undue sarcasm and downright ire.

So what's the main problem in the world today? How would someone even begin to define it? What exactly are people trying to resolve? Why are many people on edge and so stressed out? Why is such rude behavior exhibited without any shame? What about the wars, riots, and merciless acts of terrorism? People are suing each other for just about anything these days. Perhaps the more important question is, how did we get to this point?

By merely looking at the news, one would have reason to believe that things are simply unraveling at the seams. Thanks to the internet, TV, newspapers, and social media, we all have front-row seats to lawlessness, disrespect, tension, and unrest everywhere. Why is all this happening?

The answer is simple: *godlessness.*

Some say the problem is too many guns. Some say it's not enough guns. Some argue the point of mental health, single-parent upbringing, and a host of many other issues. I would simply make the suggestion that members of our society have fallen deeper into a state of despair in large part due to being void of God.

People in general don't want to hear what God has to say. They've put the Bible on the shelf or may have even thrown it away. Some believe it's old-fashioned and doesn't apply to today's complex issues. A deliberate movement away from the truths of God's biblical teachings continues, and somehow people act surprised when sinful human nature is in full display everywhere you look. Godlessness is the real problem and it manifests itself in people's behaviors all over the globe.

We were all supremely designed with a moral compass, but it's vanishing faster than we care to admit. What's worse is that godlessness is contagious and seems to be spreading at lightning speed across the societies of our world.

It's also no surprise that the media doesn't want to go anywhere near this subject. Calling out godlessness is not popular and certainly not politically correct, and is quickly swept under the rug. Someone just might get offended, and this will certainly not get the ratings up. Honestly, people don't want to hear that godlessness is the problem. That notion seems so harsh, after all.

The causes for godlessness are many. Pride, lust, greed, ego, and envy (not necessarily in that order) all for complete exposure, always lurking beneath the surface. All of us can fall victim to any or all of these destructive forces, whether we admit it or not.

Just look at the world's current state. Spousal infidelity, immorality, disrespect, stealing, lying, cheating, looting, rioting, killing, worshiping false gods, etc. abound. If left unchecked against biblical truth, our fallen human nature deceives our minds, blinds our better judgment, and quickly spirals downward toward the lowest forms of inappropriate behavior.

God has revealed Himself in the pages of the Bible for our own good. Our responsibility is to discover His true nature and heed His advice. We have to be willing to listen to what He has to say. He knows the details to the smallest and largest possible degree, so much better than we could ever fathom. His holy and perfect character is plain for us to observe, so we are all without excuse.

1 Corinthians 6:9–10 tells us, "Do you not know that the unrighteous will not inherit the kingdom of God? Do not be deceived. Neither fornicators, nor idolaters, nor adulterers, nor homosexuals, nor sodomites, nor thieves, nor covetous, nor drunkards, nor revilers, nor extortioners will inherit the kingdom of God."

People who continue to humble themselves and honestly seek the true nature of God are far from perfect. There are no ideal people who God considers sure candidates for residency in heaven. The Bible is full of individuals who committed great sins against God yet with proper repentance were forgiven, and this should give us hope.

God knows our limits and all the temptations of our human nature. He knows our hearts. He cannot be fooled by those who want to distort the plain language of His Word to custom fit their lifestyle. God didn't send Jesus to die for people who don't need help. It's quite the opposite, as God knows that we all fall short when it comes to having what it takes to inherit the kingdom of heaven on our own: "And such were some of you. But you were washed, but you were sanctified, but you were justified in the name of the Lord Jesus and by the Spirit of our God" (1 Corinthians 6:11).

Can there possibly be any better news than 1 Corinthians 6:11 for those who are imperfect (that would be all of us) and seeking to be in heaven with God? After listing the people who will not inherit the kingdom of God, the very next verse is definitive utilizing the past tense phrase: "and such *were* some of you." This means that some were cured and no longer belonged on that list. No matter what condition you currently find yourself in, there is absolute hope for you to be in heaven, so long as you earnestly and humbly ask for God's help to getting yourself off that list.

We are also told not to be deceived. No priest, counselor, fortune teller, teacher, minister, or family member—no person on earth—can possibly give us a prescription for what we need to do to inherit the kingdom of heaven. God is our only hope. Seek His advice. He is the only one who can transform your heart so that you too can be one of those who *was* on that list.

Continuing to have an inappropriate or limited understanding of God is a sure way for people to exhibit rampant godlessness. The solution, as unpopular as it may be, is for all of us to seek the Creator of the universe and get to know Him personally. The better our understanding of God's complete sovereignty, the more we realize how dependent we truly are on Him for every breath we take.

Start with humility in your heart. Do not allow pride, lust, greed, ego, and envy to control you. Instead, ask God to help you line up your will with His. With an open heart and a willingness to discover God's biblical truth, make an earnest effort to seek Him out, believe that you will find Him, and then turn away from sinful ways. By the grace of God's sacrifice of His Son Jesus, He alone can transform your heart, and then He alone will add your name to the list of citizens of heaven, and you will know it.

Reflection Questions

Can you think of bad situations in your own circle of influence where godlessness was at the root of it all?

_____
_____
_____
_____
_____
_____
_____
_____
_____
_____
_____
_____
_____

Will you help others identify the problem thus becoming a part of the solution for humanity at large?

_____
_____
_____
_____
_____
_____
_____
_____
_____
_____
_____
_____
_____

15

"RIZ" KIDS

*Fathers, do not provoke your children to anger,
but bring them up in the discipline
and instruction of the Lord.*
—Ephesians 6:4 ESV

If you're fortunate enough to have kids, you can relate to the emotional rollercoaster parents experience. Everything from the heights of pure joy all the way to down to worries and futile frustration. It's all part of parenthood, and it's because we as parents are wired with the capacity to love and care for our kids' well-being. Having kids also brings a greater sense of responsibility into the mix. Our kids may not always believe it, but we simply want them to be happy and protected from harm.

I am incredibly blessed to have witnessed the births of my amazing kids: Kyle, Kendyl, Kelly, and Katie. They're now young adults who are individual miracles, and I dedicate this chapter especially to them. In reality, they're also behind my motivation to complete this project of love for them.

My kids have learned enough about me to know that putting things in writing adds emphasis, meaning, and importance to what I'm trying to communicate. Writing creates a sort of permanent record on which you're willing to place your name. I admit that it was this sense of love and responsibility toward my kids that energized me to keep going during times when I was tempted to simply stop writing. Even though I've wandered away from biblical teaching more times than I care to remember, I want my kids to know that God forgives. I want them to know that no matter what condition they find themselves in, they can never have a more reliable and trustworthy friend than God Himself. My hope is that they each open their heart to the healing truth of His Word.

We all have personal stories with certain routines, occasional ups and downs, and unique points of view on a variety of topics. However, I would like you to take some time to think about the following questions:

- What would it be like to bring to life an idea that you thought could really have a positive impact on others around you?
- Would you be enthusiastic and take action, or would you become discouraged quickly and talk yourself out of doing anything about it? I mean, can you really imagine all the questions you'd have to answer, looking at yourself in the mirror and wondering if it might have helped, had you only bothered to try?
- How would you go about gathering the information for your presentation?
- Where would you go to obtain confirmation?
- Who would you have to convince that the assignment is really worthwhile?
- Would anyone even take the time to consider the magnitude of what you're trying to convey?

- Would anyone really care, much less appreciate your efforts? What facts and figures would you have to research to make your case good enough for it to be taken seriously?
- Whose approval would you seek before you ventured out into an unpopular and controversial topic?
- What would you do if you felt overwhelmed when faced with roadblocks and opposition?
- Would you back down or dig your heels in and move ahead?
- What about all the critics out there just waiting to discourage you every step of the way? Where would you go for guidance and encouragement?
- Who would you talk with to gain the energy needed to proceed? Would you quit before even starting the assignment, or would you reach deep into the core of your being for the conviction and endurance needed to press forward?
- Would you have the courage to defend your belief? Would you make the decision to finish the race because you believe it will help others find their way as well?

The topic is God—discovering the Creator of the universe. Everything works better when we not only acknowledge His existence but also take the time to get to know Him personally, just as we would get to know a friend of the highest possible character. As we gain understanding, we will realize that God's love for us surpasses all things. Just as all responsible parents want to teach the truth and protect their kids from harm, God wants the same for all of humanity—much more so, in fact.

My kids are all kind, funny, determined, courageous, tolerant, and even sarcastic at times. As much as I may want to protect them from the possible harms of life, I know that only God can provide the eternal protection of heaven for their eternal souls. For now, all I can do is given them some heartfelt advice:

1. Know without a doubt that you are all miracles of life with an eternal living spirit inside you. Every breath you take is a gift from the God.
2. Value time. Be kind and compassionate, and help one another—especially when it's hard.
3. Be honest, keep your word, and live with integrity. Your character will speak volumes for you.
4. Hang out with positive, can-do people without a sense of entitlement. Know that you were designed with all the tools you need to overcome any obstacle in life.
5. Learn to discern and eliminate toxic situations from your life quickly.
6. Live with courage, joy, and enthusiasm. This is a daily choice you should always make.
7. Forgive yourself when you make mistakes. Forgive others as well. Keep the lessons.
8. Stop at a kid's lemonade stand, ask the kid if it's any good, offer to pay twice the advertised price, compliment the kid for the lemonade, and then enjoy the happiness in that kid's eyes.
9. Be respectful, with a sense of gratitude and appreciation. Cash flow and leverage will also serve you well. Learn to manage money so you don't become a slave to it. Don't love money.
10. Above all things, seek God first. Acknowledge Him in every circumstance of your life. He is holy, true, sovereign, and the Creator of everything. Realize that all people are sinners and need God's forgiveness to be in His presence. Believe by faith that God's Son Jesus died in your place to pay the price for your sin. He then rose so that the eternal spirit of all who believe in Him will end up in heaven forever. Always seek biblical truth, and God will direct your steps in life. Read and heed the wisdom of the book of Solomon. You will find many priceless treasures there.

I have come to understand that there is a reason, a time, and a purpose for everything. My life has included both happy times and disappointments, and it is no accident that we're all here right now, in the exact situation we find ourselves in. No doubt, there can always be improvement. What we need to do is be willing to lose the pride, humble ourselves, and turn to our Creator for His guidance.

I am blessed that my kids have grown into healthy and beautiful young adults. I am committed to do my part, to always be truthful with them and to guide them to God's Word. They have all been designed with amazingly unique gifts and God-given natural talents. Even if their T-ball and basketball careers were temporary, it was an honor for me to have witnessed them. I love my kids more than I can express on these pages.

I'll close this chapter with advice from Ephesians 6:2–3: "'Honor your father and mother,' which is the first commandment with promise, 'that it may be well with you and you may live long on the earth.'"

Reflection Questions

What advice would you give your kids?

_____
_____
_____
_____
_____
_____
_____
_____
_____
_____
_____
_____
_____

How would you want them to remember you?

_____
_____
_____
_____
_____
_____
_____
_____
_____
_____
_____
_____
_____

16

VIDEO, AUDIO, AND THOUGHT RECORDINGS

And there is no creature hidden from His sight, but all things are naked and open to the eyes of Him to whom we must give account.
—Hebrews 4:13

$\mathcal{S}$tories are recorded daily all over the globe. We're exposed to them every time we open a newspaper, turn on the TV, or go online. Social media sites keep people in touch with friends and relatives, providing everything from legitimate celebrations to rude gossip to plain useless information. We're being told the latest in nutrition, health, business, fashion, sports, and politics. We want to know what's going on, what happened to who, and how and why.

Media is constantly vying for our attention. It's everywhere, and it's big business with mind-numbing amounts of money spent by advertisers. Local TV channels as well as national and international TV news stations continuously compete to be first in getting the latest story—the breaking news—in front of our

Citizen of Heaven

eyes and ears. Live broadcasts, interviews, reality shows, shock and awe, and raw human emotion on full display is what it's all about. After all, they're competing for precious ratings so they can make us all come back for more.

It's all fair game. What's the most newsworthy story? Is the story exaggerated in a juicy way so it sells? What kind of personality delivering the news will likely draw the biggest crowds and cause the most outrageous reaction with viewers? Big money is spent to attract us to one news agency over another. With the use of the internet, news is accessible to practically everyone as it happens in real time.

Every day, we're also bombarded with direct and indirect subliminal messages urging us to look at this and listen to that. Buy this and try that because the latest studies by "qualified experts" say so.

Looking at the magazine displays at store checkouts, one would conclude that we couldn't possibly live without knowing about this stuff—the latest socialite sighting in Hollywood, the latest diets, the secret weddings, the rumors of splits and affairs, the latest exercises, the latest fads, and of course the latest provocative moves that practically guarantee maximum human ecstasy.

We see these magazines, and our brains rationalize that we need to know more, so we buy them. After all, why would they put them right there in front of us? They must be important to our everyday lives. We don't want to miss out. We'll just put some of the magazines in the shopping cart and read the details when we get home. *Finally*, we think to ourselves, *some information I've been waiting for is available for average folks. Now this will somehow improve my life because I'll be in the know.* Yes, now we'll be happy, right?

Some stories are captivating and can make us feel sad, scared, angry, or even horrified. Others bring out feelings of joy, hope, comfort, and inspiration. They all appeal to our senses because there are real people behind them. We can relate in some way to what's being reported, so we keep reading, watching, or listening. We want to stay informed because we're wired this way.

Is anyone keeping track of all this? Is it even possible for a generation to go back and get the full story of exactly what happened? History books have been written to capture the essence of what took place in the past, but certainly with limited description of the details. Video footage of events can be pretty convincing, although it still only displays information shown from the angle of the recording lens. Audio tapes can also provide clarity, but the listener can't possibly know the thoughts and motives of the speaker. There are even social media rules and acronyms used to help prevent misunderstanding of the message being transmitted.

The short answer is a resounding *yes*. Someone is keeping track of it all.

Everything is being recorded in real time from every possible angle. Every sound and every movement made anywhere at any time by anything and by anyone is being recorded continuously. No batteries are required because God is doing all the recording. Every fraction of every second of time is captured in complete detail. The slightest of movements will be able to be played back frame by frame, from all angles, with perfect clarity. This complete recording will display in vivid color exactly what took place everywhere, including your entire life on earth, without any possibility of error. It will be the epitome of truth.

Can you imagine what it will be like, standing in front of a throne of judgment while every movement and every sound you've ever made in your life is shown to you on a large replay screen? More amazing yet will be that while you're watching and listening to the undisputable details of your actions, your thoughts and emotions will also be displayed simultaneously. This recording will highlight if you were honest and genuine, deceptive with ulterior motives, or merely choosing to go with the flow.

As this record is displayed, you will have no doubt that what you heard or read about God being perfectly just, had been true all along. You will know that the Creator of the universe is for real and He is the judge who is playing the recording right in front of you. This holy God will ask you if you know who He is, not merely if you've heard of Him. The evidence will be overwhelming and complete. With nothing hidden, will the replay of your life indicate an honest relationship with God Himself or will it not?

If you find yourself unprepared on that day, you'll realize that the concept of evolution had been nothing but a lie and you allowed yourself to be fooled. You will come face-to-face with the truth of eternal consequences, and sheer terror will engulf your soul. You will also realize that you were given many opportunities to open your heart to the God of the Bible, but you chose to ignore His mercy all along. You were too "cool" to acknowledge God. At this point, it will be too late and you will know it.

You will have nobody to blame because of the choices you made throughout your life. You might try to say that you were set up or that other people lied to you. You might try to say that you were misled or not guided in the right direction. You might even try to hang your hat on your upbringing, common popular teachings in schools, or any other circumstances you can think of. Maybe you'll try and blame some other influential people you followed for whatever reason.

Unfortunately, the detailed replay of your life will leave you without excuse for your personal disobedience to God's direction. Your thoughts, your words, your conduct, and your actions will leave you with no doubt as to where you stand. You will be held accountable for the choices you've made. If you take your last breath here on earth without having asked for and received the forgiveness of the Creator, you will find yourself in front of God's White Throne of Judgment with no way to dispute the undeniable recorded evidence against you. The true condition of your heart will be revealed, as God cannot be fooled.

The good news is that if you're reading these words right now, you still have the opportunity to make things right. Take the time to get to know the Creator of the universe while you're here on earth. Humble yourself and ask Him to reveal Himself to you.

Reflection Questions

Do you realize that nothing can be hidden from God?

Will you ask God to help you line up your will with His going forward? Will you ask Him to forgive you and guide you going forward?

17

FOREVER—IT'S CRITICAL

For the wages of sin is death, but the gift of God is eternal life in Christ Jesus our Lord.
—*Romans 6:23*

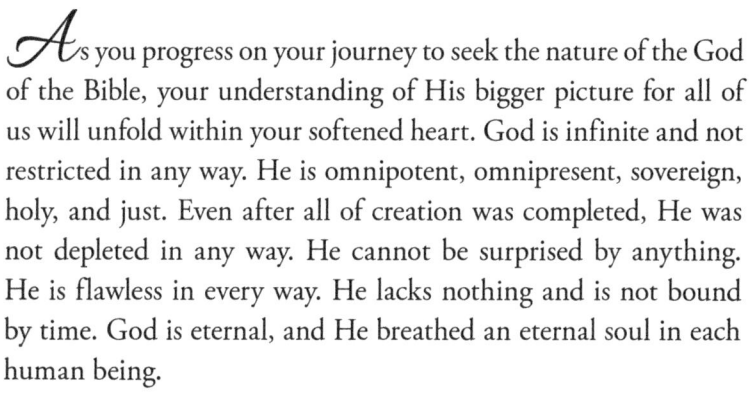

*A*s you progress on your journey to seek the nature of the God of the Bible, your understanding of His bigger picture for all of us will unfold within your softened heart. God is infinite and not restricted in any way. He is omnipotent, omnipresent, sovereign, holy, and just. Even after all of creation was completed, He was not depleted in any way. He cannot be surprised by anything. He is flawless in every way. He lacks nothing and is not bound by time. God is eternal, and He breathed an eternal soul in each human being.

As such, to end up in His holy presence, our eternal souls need to be forgiven and saved from eternal death. This need for forgiveness is often misunderstood, as most people think of themselves as "pretty good people." Surely God would allow their eternal souls into heaven, right? I mean, what do we all have to be forgiven for anyway?

Romans 3:23 answers that question: "For all have sinned and fall short of the glory of God." In short, we need to be forgiven for our sinful nature as mortal human beings. We have to be forgiven for rejecting God's laws and making up our own, which feel better to us. We choose to live our lifestyles the way we please and ignore God's will.

Have you ever told a little white lie? Have you ever taken something—even something as insignificant as a paper clip—that doesn't belong to you? Have you ever lusted in your heart over someone? Every single person on earth is guilty to some extent. Left alone to our own will, we all rebel against God's perfect nature and His laws. All of humanity has sinned against Him ever since Adam and Eve. Satan is the source of all sin in our lives, as we allow him to deceive us away from God's laws.

Can you imagine being in the presence of a holy God who knows you and then asking Him to let you into heaven because you're a "pretty good person," yet you have virtually no idea who God is? It's just not going to happen, so don't fool yourself. Going through the motions of acknowledging God's existence isn't good enough either. God is holy. The penalty for sin is death, and the price must be paid because God is also perfectly just.

It is simply impossible for anyone to ask for genuine forgiveness from God—to be pardoned from the punishment of death—unless that person is convicted of their sinful nature against God Himself. If anyone truly looked to gain understanding of God's holiness, they would come face-to-face with their own depravity and understand that they're deserving of God's wrath. It is only then that the person realizes that they need forgiveness to escape eternal death.

Search your heart honestly, realize that God already knows you better than you know yourself, and then humble yourself and ask for God's forgiveness and His guidance going forward. Once you have arrived at the realization that your eternal soul has no hope of entering heaven without God's forgiveness, the sincerity of your request for forgiveness will actually matter to Him.

So if the wages of sin is death, and God is a perfect and just God, then someone had to have paid the price of sin by dying. We all deserved to die due to our sinful nature, but God showed unfathomable mercy toward us. His plan for our salvation from eternal death was to send His only Son Jesus from heaven to earth and be born of Virgin Mary. Jesus lived a sinless life among the people of the earth, then was betrayed and crucified in our place to satisfy God's wrath.

The Bible teaches that God's Son Jesus, who had no sin, was the only one who could have paid this price by dying in our place and then rising from the dead on the third day, conquering death itself. This amazing act of God's love was and continues to be His greatest gift to mankind. God offers this gift *free* for us to receive, but the price paid could not have been any greater. We who believe are indebted to Jesus due to the sacrifice He paid on our behalf, far beyond our human comprehension.

John 14:6 says, "Jesus answered, 'I am the way the truth and the life. No one comes to the Father except through Me'" (NIV). It all boils down to this simple yet critical belief. We can obtain forgiveness of our sins, get saved from eternal death in hell, and receive eternal life in heaven by believing in Jesus, who undeservedly paid the ultimate price in our place. Jesus is the only reason we can have access to heaven.

Every person on earth will ultimately either believe that the God of the Bible exists, or believe that He does not exist. This topic cannot be avoided, as it dwells deep within all human beings regardless of their views and opinions. If you believe that God exists, then you must also believe in the biblical teachings of a real place called heaven and a real place called hell where the eternal souls of humanity will end up.

Our individual eternal destiny in heaven all starts and ends with our personal relationship with God Himself. You either believe the God of the Bible created everything, or you do not. You either believe that God's only Son Jesus paid the ultimate sacrifice in your place so your eternal soul could be in God's presence, or you do not. There is no gray area. There is nothing more important than spending eternity—forever—in heaven.

As John 11:26 says, "And whoever lives and believes in Me will never die. Do you believe this?"

Reflection Questions

Do you believe that you can end up in eternal heaven by being forgiven and saved by God's grace, through faith in God's son Jesus?

_____
_____
_____
_____
_____
_____
_____
_____
_____
_____
_____
_____
_____

If so, are you willing to tell others about it?

_____
_____
_____
_____
_____
_____
_____
_____
_____
_____
_____
_____
_____

18

SARCASM—OFFEND SOMEONE YOU CARE ABOUT

Where were you when I laid the foundations of the earth? Tell Me, if you have understanding. Who determined its measurements? Surely you know! Or who stretched the line upon it? To what were its foundations fastened? Or who laid its cornerstone?
—*Job 38:4–6*

The book of Job is one of enormous significance. Although Job knew God and was an upright man in the sight of God, he was tested in ways that would be difficult for the average person to imagine. God allowed a series of devastating events to take place in Job's life. While Job continued to worship God, he also wondered what he had done wrong to deserve such afflictions and misfortunes. In their exchange, God ultimately asked him a series of questions, essentially putting Job in his rightful place. God was saying that there was a much bigger plan, outside of what was obviously happening, that Job could not even begin to understand. Job ultimately conceded and their relationship was restored.

We may come from different nations with unique backgrounds, but we all have red blood running through our veins to sustain life in our bodies. We all have feelings, a conscience, and an intricate brain to help us think for ourselves regardless of anything that is happening around us. We know right from wrong. We can choose to build or destroy, empower or suppress, encourage or ridicule, love or hate, enrich or hurt, move forward or remain stagnant, or speak truthfully or be deceitful.

We were all created in God's image—by Him and for Him. Everything and everyone belongs to Him since He is the Creator of everything that exists. God is the OEM (original equipment manufacturer) of everything. He also wrote the manual—the Bible—that spells out everything from how it all started to how it will all finish. This manual is so complete, it affords the reader (us) the ability to get to know the essence and character of God in great detail, the maintenance needed for everything to function as intended, and the warnings of consequences if we deviate. We may not all be willing to do this, but God certainly has the right to expect us to follow His laws. They were spelled out for our own good.

Don't touch the stove. Don't play with matches. Don't run in the street. These are just a few of the many warnings we give our kids early in life. We don't want them to get hurt. We care about their well-being. Hopefully, our kids will mature enough over time to appreciate our responsibility as parents. Hopefully, they will eventually realize that even though they may not have liked our answers when they were young, we gave those answers because we were caring parents. We simply want them to trust our judgment and heed our warnings, especially in the early years when their lives are so dependent on us.

As adults we become less and less dependent on our parents, but most of us fail to realize our continued dependence on God Himself. We tend to dismiss Him altogether. We think we've got life all figured out with our jobs, our families, our friends, and all our stuff. We're self-sufficient and just want to do our own thing, expressing ourselves in our own individuality. We believe we're not sick at all, so what on earth would we need to be saved from? We ignore God's manual because we would rather adjust His guidance, overrule His laws, and make our own rules as we see fit, to make ourselves feel better about our decisions.

In the meantime, we continue to depend on the sun to keep coming up at the same time every day. We continue to depend on the attraction of the moon to churn the oceans. We continue to depend on the earth to rotate on its axis and revolve around the sun at constant speeds. We continue to depend on our hearts to keep pumping blood. And we continue to depend on our lungs to keep bringing oxygen to our brains while we're sleeping.

Have we, as intelligent people, figured out all these miracles that all of humanity depends on every single moment? Have we figured out the source of the forces that sustain life all around us? At this point, whether you are a God-fearing person or not is irrelevant because most of us take these things for granted. God continues to extend His grace and mercy by allowing everyone to benefit from His amazing creation, whether we admit it or not. After centuries and gazillions of dollars spent on deep-space exploration, extensive medical science, and DNA evidence development (just to name a few), are we any closer to admitting that a supernatural God not only created it all, but also sustains it in ways that are humanly impossible to understand? *No.*

Why do we, as the product of God's creation, continue to expect Him to explain Himself to us until we like the answers? It's probably because we don't care enough to get to know His perfect and holy nature that would put Him far above our understanding. Without knowing who He is, we can't possibly begin to admit, much less appreciate, that He's in complete control of everything, while we are but dust by comparison. We're sadly too full of ourselves, and we make no room for God in our lives. We refuse to gain understanding of His sovereignty, and as such remain in the dark about the truth of His grandeur. We just don't want to be held accountable.

We're hypocrites. Our sinful nature has blinded us to the point that we simply refuse to develop any meaningful relationship with the God of the universe, yet we walk around on *His* property and fly around in *His* air space every day, full of pride. We spend more time researching what some movie star's favorite color may be, or what they like to eat for breakfast, or what their *sign* really means, as if this is somehow important. No doubt, God is patient beyond description with us, but only to a point.

Having various disagreements on trivial things with someone you know and care about will probably not make any difference at all. You both realize that it really doesn't matter that you disagree on these minor subjects, so you decide to leave it at that. However, if the different points of view being expressed—such as who God is—have significant eternal consequences for your friend or family member, what path will you choose then? Will you say something? *I might offend them, after all*, you think. *It's their point of view anyway, so who am I to interfere?*

Do you even know enough about God to recognize the significance of your friend or family member's misunderstanding? Will you care enough to tell them the truth (in love) even if they might be offended? You may find that they'll admit to you that they really didn't know for sure, and they may even thank you for pointing it out. If you're fortunate enough to have a personal relationship with God, then you ought to care enough to share with that other person the truth about His character above all things. This sharing of biblical truth will show you really care about the other person's well-being, whether they heed your advice or not.

Some time ago, I ended up in a conversation with a young lady who claimed to be a Christian. I recall saying something like, "That's great. So am I." She continued by saying that the Christian belief is in Jesus Christ, God's Son, who died for our sins, but some of her friends had different beliefs about access to heaven. I then asked her if she personally believed that both she and her friends would ultimately end up in heaven.

She told me that "Yeah, probably" they would all be in heaven, mostly because she and her friends are all good people. She later explained that she wasn't really sure herself, nor did she really think about the subject, but she was "pretty sure" God would allow them all in heaven. She also didn't feel comfortable saying anything to her friends that would appear to be a judgment on her friends' faith. She was a pleasant young lady but could not speak with conviction because she lacked a personal relationship with the God of the Bible.

Shortly afterward, I mentioned something about the need for all of us to increase our understanding of God, who is the only one who can provide access to heaven. At first, this young lady seemed somewhat offended. I did my best to explain to her that I cared enough to share the truth about God and the Bible's teaching about access to heaven. When we parted ways, she still seemed surprised by my statement that we show our love for our friends by sharing biblical truth. Hopefully she cared enough to continue to seek Him for herself and know for sure in order to share it with her friends.

Another interaction took place recently with a young man of about twenty-four years who was a waiter at a small restaurant where I was having dinner. Making small talk, he said something about the crazy events in the world these days. My response to him was that godlessness was certainly running rampant. He wasn't offended, but he was certainly surprised by my comment. He went on to indicate that there could be a god out there because this god must have been behind the scene when evolution first began billions and billions of years ago.

My heart went out to this young man, so I asked if he could imagine a forest of trees ever becoming the wooden frame of a house, without any human intervention, no matter how much time passed by. He smiled and said, "There's no way." I agreed and then asked him if, once built, he thought the wooden frame would have any idea that some human being had designed and built it. "Of course not," he replied.

Then I commented about how much more difficult it would be for specific organs not only to appear fully developed, from nothing, but also to assemble themselves into a functioning human being, all by chance and without any form of outside intervention.

Just as it took human intelligence to cut the forest trees and assemble the wooden frame of the house, the human body had to have had supernatural intelligence design and assemble all its components too. Just as the wooden frame had no idea how it was shaped and put together by the human being, we also have no understanding of how we as humans were formed and brought to life, other than what God who created us revealed in the Bible. He supernaturally spoke everything into existence and breathed life into us.

The young man didn't dismiss anything we talked about. Instead, he seemed to listen with curiosity as we talked for a couple more minutes, then he admitted that he had very limited knowledge of both God and evolution. He appreciated our short interaction and said that he'd look into it further because it seemed important. He originally claimed that there was nothing after this life on earth. Following our conversation, he was willing to learn more about the reality of God, heaven, and hell.

Give yourself a chance to learn who God is, then go ahead and offend someone you care about. They just might thank you.

Reflection Questions

Will you engage in a conversation about God's love and mercy with someone who doesn't believe?

_____
_____
_____
_____
_____
_____
_____
_____
_____
_____
_____
_____

Do you realize that this is showing the other person that you really care?

_____
_____
_____
_____
_____
_____
_____
_____
_____
_____
_____
_____

19

APPLICATION FOR CITIZENSHIP

Trust in the LORD with all your heart, and lean not on your own understanding. In all your ways acknowledge Him, and He shall direct your paths.
—*Proverbs 3:5–6*

*N*o doubt, we're all creatures of habit. Most people don't readily embrace change. We get comfortable in our routines and don't want to be bothered by even thinking of something different.

If we catch a cold or get some minor scratchiness in our throat, we count on some common over-the-counter medication. Other than that, most people are typically healthy and not usually prepared for out-of-the-ordinary emergencies. Obviously, we're glad the hospitals, doctors, and nurses are available, but we don't necessarily believe we'll need them, especially if life goes on day after day in a normal fashion.

Sure, fatal accidents happen all the time, but we normally hear about these events on the news. Somehow, it doesn't really register that it could actually happen to any of us at any given moment.

If we really did believe that we were in some type of danger, then logic would set in and cause us to react immediately. We would likely drop everything we're doing and focus on getting prepared to eliminate the hazard or fight the illness to the best of our ability.

The normalcy bias can be described as a mental state people enter when facing a pending disaster. It causes people to underestimate the possibility of danger because they have a bias to believe that things will always function the way things normally function. An example of this is a frog swimming around in a container of cool water. If the container of water is slowly heated on a stovetop, the frog will continue to swim around because it doesn't realize the danger it's in. The frog's body temperature will slowly rise along with the water temperature until it's too late for the frog to jump out. The frog will eventually pass out and die.

In a similar way, life happens all around us as time rolls right along. Day after day, we go about our business, taking time to eat, sleep, work, exercise, spend time with family, socialize with friends, play games, watch favorite TV shows, attend entertainment events, and perhaps even attend church services. Life becomes somewhat routine for us. Our calendars are full. Given all of what we're occupied with, it's safe to say that a relatively small percentage of our time is spent thinking about the miracle of God being in our midst, and even less time is spent dwelling on His character.

The truth is that few people make a point to meet with God for His daily guidance, for any appreciable length of time, because we're "very busy." What should we talk about anyway? We also rarely show adequate appreciation of Him for the daily routines and liberties we've become so accustomed to enjoying. Even if we consider the benefits of regular interactions with God, we simply put it off for a later time when it's more convenient. Perhaps when we're older and closer to the end of our life expectancy, we'll spend more time with God. We procrastinate because we don't believe we're in any sort of immediate danger. We've become accustomed to our normalcy bias.

Jeremiah 9:23–24 tells us, "Thus says the LORD: 'Let not the wise man glory in his wisdom, let not the mighty man glory in his might, let not the rich man glory in his riches; but let him who glories glory in this, that he understands and knows Me, that I am the LORD, exercising lovingkindness, judgment, and righteousness in the earth. For in these I delight.'"

In addition to being a citizen of the country you were born in, you may want to become a citizen of a different country. If you want to become a citizen of Canada or the United States, or any other country on earth, you will look into the respective laws and requirements of that country. You'll submit your written application along with all the necessary fees, then a vetting process usually takes place. Assuming you qualify, you may wait about five years before you're accepted as a citizen.

I was born a Romanian citizen. After arriving in Canada as a young boy, I learned and obeyed the Canadian laws, applied for citizenship, paid the fees, waited about five years, and then was granted Canadian citizenship. I have recently applied for and was granted United States residency. After learning and obeying the U.S. laws, I submitted the application complete with the appropriate fees. I am currently waiting the minimum five-year period before I can apply for U.S. citizenship.

As for the application for citizenship in heaven, there's no piece of paper with a bunch of questions that you need to answer. There are no fees to pay up front because Jesus paid the price on your behalf. Once approved with a humble heart, there is no waiting period either, and there are no other prerequisites nor prequalification clauses. No person on earth, regardless of background or status or skin color, has more of a right to be in heaven than anyone else. This application is simply the act of seeking the one and only true God of the Bible who alone can grant access to heaven.

You're expected to look into it and learn about who God is since He's in charge up there. You're expected to get to know Him personally. You're expected to learn and obey the laws associated with heaven since God is holy and He makes the rules. Once you begin your pursuit, you will get to the point in your understanding of who God is and you will recognize your sinful nature. With this profound understanding, you will have the need to ask Him for forgiveness and will discover a trustworthy friend in the process. You'll then be granted instant citizenship to heaven and you will know it. There is no waiting period.

Every new day is another day of grace from God. With every new breath we take, He is giving us another opportunity to learn about His holy character and understand that He is merciful, righteous, just, and everlasting. The Creator of the universe has revealed Himself in all that exists around us, and He deserves all the glory for all of creation. He owns it all. He is worthy of our time, our appreciation, our praise, our obedience, and our worship today and every day.

The application for citizenship in heaven is an ongoing process. It is not merely acknowledging God's existence on Sundays. Every day, you fill out this application by leaving your personal DNA in all your thoughts, words, and actions. Whether you're filling out this application or not manifests itself for all to see in the way you live your life. Are you pursuing an honest relationship with the Creator of the universe? Are you willing to humble yourself, turn away from sinful ways, and seek His guidance for your life? Every day that goes by, you are either filling out the application for access to heaven or you are not.

I've heard it said that the most debilitating word in the English language is *tomorrow*. Somehow, we believe that we can put things off until later. We may even try to ignore the subject altogether, just so we can continue living in our prideful ways. It's human nature. *What's the rush anyway?* we mistakenly reason with ourselves.

We certainly don't see the urgency for getting to know God being announced on the evening news. Even people with their own TV talk shows don't bring it up. Yet these same news agencies continue to report on the horrific daily events happening across the globe, seemingly surprised, while jumping over each other to interview "experts" for explanations and answers as to why these things happen.

What do you think would happen if the news reporter would suggest, on national TV, that the main reason for these atrocities is that people have a sinful rebellious nature and most are void of God? What if the reporter continued by saying that most people simply don't know who God is, because if they did, there would be fewer and fewer of these terrible news stories to report on? Do you think the people in the background monitoring every word being said would immediately stop the broadcast? Do you think that reporter would keep his or her job afterward? More importantly, do you think the reporter would be correct in assessing the problem?

Where you stand absolutely matters. You need to have the right perspective and understanding of the grandeur of who God is, as well as the right view of who you are, as one who He created. Of all the people who ever walked the face of this earth, I am the least deserving of God's mercy. It is only by God's grace alone, through faith alone, in Jesus alone, that I was forgiven and granted immediate citizenship to heaven.

Sadly, it seems that fewer and fewer people across the globe are filling out applications for admission into heaven. Most people's lives are void of God. Fewer people are actively seeking the God of the Bible, His attributes, and His guidance. Fewer people are talking about the incredible significance of this phenomenon, its negative effects on individual behavior, and the downward spiral of society. Yet even though these signs are everywhere, even though people are openly rejecting God's biblical teachings, He continues to provide His amazing grace, looking to save those who actively seek Him.

- If you believe by faith that the God of the Bible is the one who created all celestial bodies of the heavens as well as all

that exists everywhere, by supernaturally speaking them all into existence;
- If you believe that God is omnipotent, omniscient, omnipresent, holy, sovereign, everlasting, and perfectly just;
- If you believe that God is the only one who sustains everything including the sun, the moon, our unique planet Earth, and all life on it;
- If you believe that God's Word is true, sufficient, complete, and written for our good;
- If you believe that God has a purpose for everything and He created all human beings in His likeness with a free will and an eternal soul;
- If you believe that humanity's nature became sinful starting with the disobedience of Adam and Eve, and if left alone in this fallen state, we cannot be in the presence of God;
- If you believe that it was by God's grace alone that He sent His Son Jesus, who descended to earth some two thousand years ago from the glory of heaven, to die and pay the ultimate price for man's debt due to sin;
- If you believe that God's Son Jesus undeservedly suffered, died in our place, and then rose from the dead on the third day to save us from God's justified wrath;
- If you believe that Jesus' sacrifice is the only reason we can have access to God in heaven; and
- If you believe that you need to repent for your sinful nature against the holy God, and put your trust in Jesus who paid the price in full for you, and you could never pay Him back… then you're on the right track.

You're filling out your application for citizenship to heaven, so keep learning about God's truth. Ask God to forgive you while you still have breath on earth. Put your faith in the work of Jesus, and ask for His daily guidance. Ask Him to come into your life to transform your heart. Seek Him, learn about His character, and develop a personal relationship with Him so that you know Him as you would a true friend. He will pick you up when you fall, guide you, and forgive you, and you will know for sure that you've been granted citizenship in heaven, without any waiting period.

If you have any questions or comments, or you're still not sure about God's gift of salvation, or would like to share your personal journey toward citizenship in heaven, feel free to email me at cornel@rizea-books.com. I would love to hear from you.

MAY THE GOD OF HEAVEN DRAW YOU NEAR TO HIM!

Printed in the USA
CPSIA information can be obtained
at www.ICGtesting.com
JSHW012135201223
54060JS00011B/118

9 781732 180703